THE PROVERBS CHRONICLES
Aligning Your Character with the Book of Wisdom

Copyright © 2017 by Delbra Brown
All rights reserved.

The Proverbs Life Guide is a trademark of D.A. Brown Consulting dba Hoosevents LLC

All rights reserved. No part of this book may be reproduced in any form or by any means electronic or mechanical, without prior written consent of the publisher except for the inclusion of brief quotes in a review.

Printed in the United States of America

ISBN-10:0-9990738-4-2
ISBN-13:978-0-9990738-4-1

Published by Hoosevents, LLC dba D.A. Brown Consulting
www.DABrownConsulting.com

Cake Chronicles Coaching 80/20 Life/Relationship services provided by
Delbra Brown
Rochester NY 14606
(585) 317-4313
Delbra@CakeChroniclescom
Delbra@DABrownConsulting.com

Discount pricing offered to educational and organizational institutions that desire to use this self-help guide in volume or a group setting. Contact Mrs. Brown for details on volume pricing.

Copyrighted Material

Copyright 2018 The Proverbs Chronicles
Aligning your Character with the Book of Wisdom

All rights reserved. No part of this book may be used or reproduced, stored in a retrieval system, or transmitted in any form or by any means, graphics, or electronics, or mechanical, including photocopying, recording, taping or by any information storage retrieval system without the written permission.

Hoosevents, LLC dba D.A. Brown Consulting
Rochester, New York
(585) 317-4313

SCRIPTURE TRANSLATIONS

Used throughout the Book

ASV – American Standard Version
BBE – Bible in Basic English
CEB – Common English Bible
CSB – Holman Christian Standard
ERV – Easy To Read Version
ESV – English Standard Version
GNT – Good News Translation
GW – God's Word Translation
HNV – Hebrew Names Version
KJV – King James Version
MSG – The Message
NAS – New American Standard
NCV – New Century Standard
NIRV – New International Reader's Version
NIV – New International Version
NKJ – New King James
NLT – New Living Translation
NRS – New Revised Standard
TNIV – Today's New International Version

MY MOTIVATION

My grandmother IS a force to be reckoned with. I say IS because whether she's here on earth in the flesh, or up in Heaven with God, Jesus, the angels and the other family members that have preceded her in death, she will FOREVER be present and alive through me and her descendants. One day while sitting in church, as the pastor asked us to turn to a scripture in the Bible; I noticed she had a photo of me when I was five (5) years old tucked in between the pages of her Bible. When I asked her to turn back and let me take a look, she just shrugged off my gesture and shushed me so we could hear the pastor's sermon. Over the years, I would wonder I why I could never get away with the things that most people could get away with. Over the years, I realized it was because my grandmother ensured the Lord's hedge of protection was covering me, all the days of my life. The goal of this guide is to help believers work daily to ensure their character lines up with God's desire for our lives. May this bless you in the same way it blessed me to study God's words for our lives.

ABOUT THE AUTHOR

I do not claim to be an expert in religion, psychology, or counseling, but experience has taught me a lot about all three. 2 Timothy 2:15 says: "Study to show thyself approved unto God, a workman that needeth not be ashamed, rightly dividing the Word of truth." I was born in Rochester, New York. My family didn't go to church at all until I was almost in my late teens/early twenties because unfortunately for me, our family was living their lives as Carnal Minded Christians. Growing up I always knew there was something "special" about me but like many others, I could never put my finger on exactly what "it" was. I knew I was not gifted as an entertainer or athlete so I knew I would not impact the world in those arena's. Growing up in a family where there was competition amongst family members, anger, contention, lack of trust and even a lack of respect, I knew this was not good and I didn't want any part of it, but I didn't know what "different" looked like. I continued to go to church and the more I heard the word, the more I started learning what "different" could look like. I knew it wouldn't be easy because it was something I had never tried before but what I did know, was that something had to change in my life, and in me. I stayed at that church for a few years until I started realizing year after year I kept hearing the same messages from the same books of the bible. I was ready for more, but I didn't know how to obtain it. One day while studying the book of Proverbs, I noticed the outline in my book provided an overview of how Proverbs referenced wisdom and character. Many years later, I decided to write this book; a reference guide of how our character and desire to be wise can be found in the scriptures outlined in Proverbs. Solomon asked God for wisdom and if we align our actions according to the Proverbs, we can stand on the word of truth when it comes to accepting and receiving honesty and correction from others. May this book challenge you to become all that God desires for you and your life by trusting and believing the word to be the author of your faith and your actions to yourself and others.

OUTLINE

About The Book of Knowledge..11
- Who Is God? (The Father, The Son, The Holy Spirit)...............12
- What is the Bible - The Old Testament..13
- What is the Bible - People in the Bible.......................................14
- What is the Bible - The New Testament......................................15
- What is the Bible - What are the Ten (10) Commandments...........16
- Fellowship with other Believers...17
- What is Prayer...18
- What is Sin?..19
- KEEP, START, STOP..20

Why Study the Book of Proverbs.................................21
- The 7 Principles for obtaining Wisdom from the Lord............22-23
- The Natural Man...24
- The Carnal Man..25
- The Spiritual Man..26

The 7 Principles for obtaining Wisdom from the Lord...27
- The 7 Principles for obtaining Wisdom from the Lord............28-29
- Knowledge of the Lord (I—III)..30-32
- Fear of the Lord (I—III)...33-35
- Mindful of the Lord..36
- Understand the Lord...37
- Trust/Acceptance of the Lord..38
- Obedience to the Lords will..39

Character of the Spiritual Man.................................43
- You're slow to become Angry 44
- You Apologize/Repent..45
- You're Appreciative/Thankful..46
- You're Calm..47
- You're Caring..48
- You're Cautious...49
- You're Confident..50
- You're Considerate...51
- You're Courageous...52

OUTLINE

Character of the Spiritual Man *(continued)*

- You're Dependable..53
- You're Diligent/Hard Worker..54
- You have Discernment..55
- You receive Discipline/Correction...56
- You show Empathy...57
- You Encourage Others..58
- You're Fair..59
- You're Financially Conscience (I—VI)............................60-65
- You're Forgiving..66
- You're Friendly..67
- You're Giving/Generous..68
- You're Helpful...69
- You're Honest/Truthful (I—II)...70-71
- You're Honorable...72
- You're Humble...73
- You have Integrity...74
- You're Joyful...75
- You use good Judgment...76
- You're Kind..77
- You're a Leader (I—III)..78-80
- You're Loving..81
- You're Mindful...82
- You're Modest/Discrete...83
- You're Patient..84
- You're Peaceful/Quiet..85
- You Persevere..86

OUTLINE

Character of the Spiritual Man *(continued)*

- You're a Planner..87
- You're Positive/Cheerful..88
- You're a Provider..89
- You're Respectful..90
- You're Righteous (I—VI)...91-96
- You show Self-Control...97
- You're Teachable/Receive Counsel (I—III)................98-100
- You Think before you Act..101
- You Think before you Speak...102
- You're Trusting..103
- You're Understanding...104
- Your Words have the power to heal..................................105
- Your Words should be few, not many...............................106
- Healthy Emotions of the Spiritual Man (Example)............107

Character of the Natural/Carnal Man......................111

- You take Advantage of People..112
- You get Angry/Irate...113
- You're Argumentative..114
- You're Arrogant/Boastful/Proud (I—II).......................115-116
- You're a Cheat..117
- You Lack Self-Control/Discipline......................................118
- You refuse Counsel/Correction...119
- You lack Direction/Motivation...120
- You're Deceptive/Manipulative...121
- You're Envious/Jealous..122
- You Exaggerate..123
- You're Foolish (I—IV)...124-127

OUTLINE

Character of the Natural/Carnal Man *(continued)*

- You Gossip/ Reveal Secrets...128
- You're Greedy/Never Satisfied..129
- You hold a Grudge...130
- You're Hot/Quick Tempered...131
- You hurt Innocent People..132
- You're Impatient..133
- You Impose/A Meddler...134
- You Instigate Trouble/Troublemaker/Vindictive (I—III)..........135-137
- You get Intoxicated/Drunk..138
- You're Judgmental..139
- You're Lazy (I—II)...140-141
- You're a Liar...142
- You break Laws..143
- You're Mean/Hateful..144
- You're Promiscuous/a Loose Woman (I—II)...........................145-146
- You're Rude..147
- You're Selfish/Stingy..148
- You're Spiteful..149
- You're Stubborn..150
- You're a Thief...151
- You can't be Trusted..152
- You're Violent..153
- You're Weak...154
- You're Wicked (I—VIII)..155-162
- Your Words have the power to Wound..163
- You Worry..164
- Natural/Carnal Unhealthy Emotions (Example).................................165

OUTLINE

Your Relationship With Your Wife.................................169
- You don't commit Adultery/Faithful (I—IV)......................170-173
- You Appreciate Her...174
- You see her as a crowning glory..175
- You're a Leader/Involved..176
- You Praise Her...177
- You Trust Her..178
- You're Respected..179

Your Relationship With Your Husband.......................183
- You're a Blessing..184
- You're a Caretaker..185
- You're Caring/Helpful..186
- You're Not a Nag...187
- You're Discrete..188
- You Fear the Lord..189
- You're Gracious...190
- Your Hard Working/Diligent..191
- You're Honorable...192
- You're Kind..193
- You're not Promiscuous (I—II)......................................194-195
- You're a Provider/Resourceful...196
- You're Respected..197
- You're Righteous...198
- You're Strong..199
- You're Trustworthy..200
- You're Virtuous/Noble...201

OUTLINE

Your Relationship With Your Children..................205
- You Discipline them with Physical/Verbal correction..............206
- You leave an Inheritance...207
- You Provide for their Physical needs.................................208
- You Provide for their Spiritual growth...............................209
- They Respect You..210
- You Teach/Train Them 211

Your Relationship With Your Parents..................215
- by being Diligent/Working Hard.......................................216
- You Listen to Them..217
- being Righteous...218
- You Receive their Correction/Discipline...........................219
- You don't Steal from Them...220
- You Take Care of Them..221

Your Relationship With Others..........................225
- You choose them Wisely...226
- You're their Companions..227
- You're Considerate...228
- You Counsel Them..229
- You're Helpful..230
- You're not Deceptive..231
- You're Honest with them..232
- You don't Lie against them...233
- You don't lend or borrow Money......................................234
- You're willing to Nurture Others......................................235
- You Value them..236
- You're Violent..237
- Your words have the power to Wound..............................238

About the Book of Knowledge & Wisdom

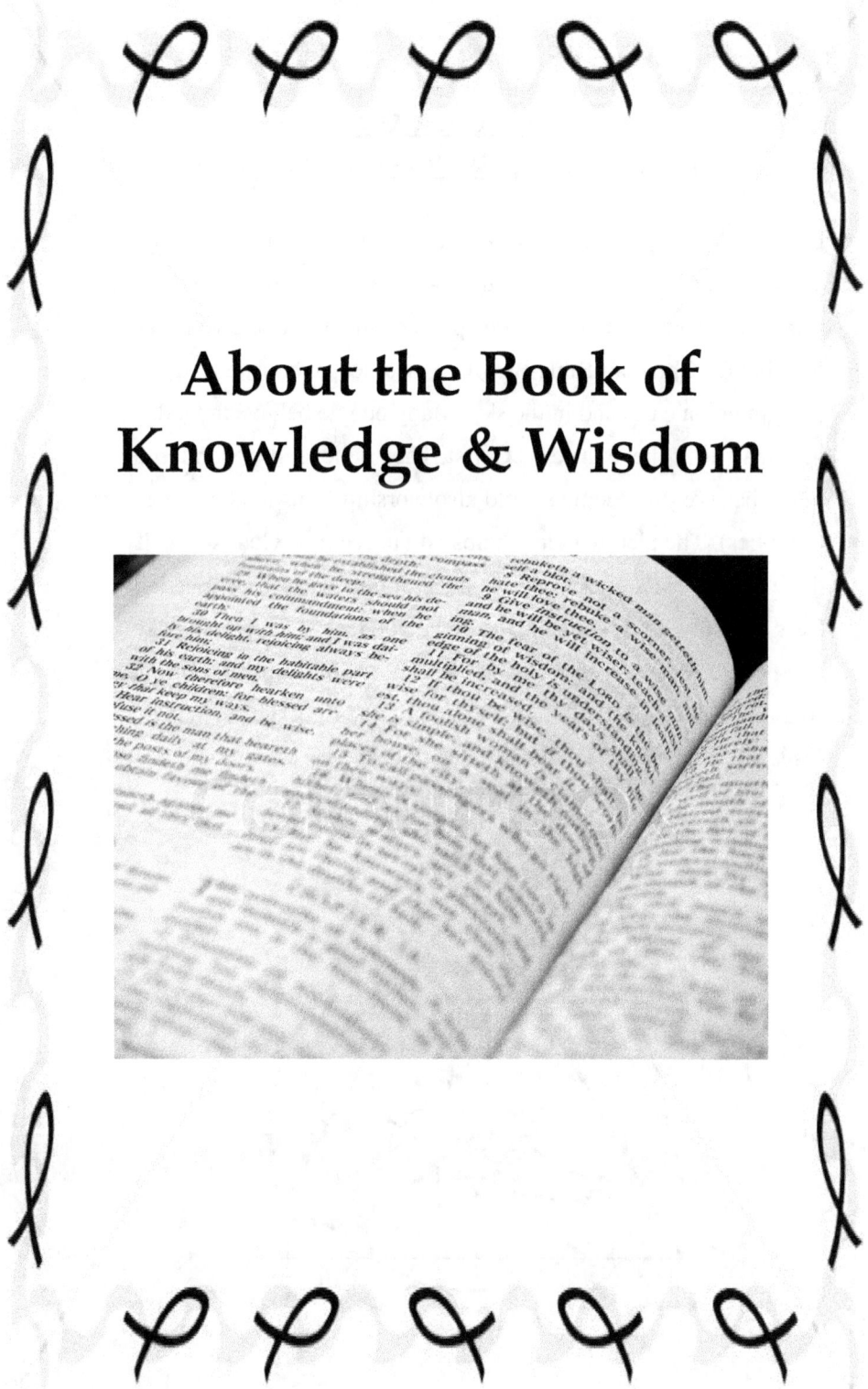

ABOUT THE BOOK OF KNOWLEDGE & WISDOM

WHO IS GOD?
THE FATHER, THE SON, & THE HOLY SPIRIT

Because America is a country with many different nationalities and religious beliefs, we forget that not everyone believes in the same God as you. There are some people who don't believe He is real, but for Christian Bible Believing people, we believe God made everything on earth and in the sky. Many people believe in God, but they may not believe in Jesus Christ. They believe in God, but they might believe that people should also worship Jesus mother (those are Catholics). The picture below helps you to see how God is actually three people. He's the Father. He's the Son name Jesus Christ, and He's the Holy Spirit which is the voice you hear to help you make good choices over bad choices. God sent his Son Jesus here on earth so that we can see how to live a life doing the right things. When Jesus died and went back to Heaven, God said He would send a comforter to be with us and that comforter is the Holy Spirit.

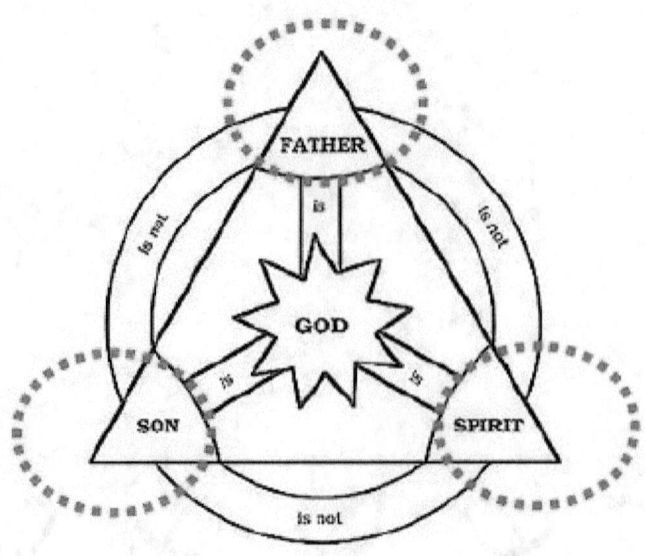

ABOUT THE BOOK OF KNOWLEDGE & WISDOM

WHAT IS THE BIBLE?
OLD TESTAMENT

The Old Testament is a collection of 39 books. It records God's interaction with mankind before He sent His son to redeem us, while recording prophesy predicting that coming. The books in the Old Testament are grouped into 5 categories:

The Pentateuch

The name means "Five Books", and this group is made up of the following books: ***Genesis, Exodus, Leviticus, Numbers*** and ***Deuteronomy***. The group is sometimes called the "Law of Moses" or the "Torah", a Hebrew word referring to God's Law or teachings.

The Historical Books

This group is made up of following books: ***Joshua, Judges, Ruth, 1st& 2nd Samuel, 1st& 2nd Chronicles, Ezra, Nehemiah and Esther.*** Together, the Pentateuch and the Historical books tell the history of Israel two times. The books of Genesis through 2nd Kings tell the history the first time. While the books of 1st Chronicles through Nehemiah tell it the second time from a somewhat different point of view.

The Poetic Books

This group is sometimes called the "Wisdom Books" and contains ***Job, Psalms, Proverbs, Ecclesiastes*** and the ***Song of Songs***. Lamentations is also one of the poetic books, but in English bibles it follows Jeremiah, because Jeremiah tells it the 2nd time from a somewhat different point of view.

The Four (4) Major Prophets

God selected four people to speak on His behalf to His people. He gave them a message to share with His people. Because God spoke directly to them, there were called Prophets. They are the longer books in the Bible and are ***Isaiah, Jeremiah, Ezekiel*** and ***Daniel***

The Minor Prophets

These books are shorter in content and were written in ***Hosea, Joel, Amos, Obadiah, Johan, Micah, Nahum, Habakkuk, Zephaniah, Haggai, Zechariah*** and ***Malachi***.

ABOUT THE BOOK OF KNOWLEDGE & WISDOM

WHAT IS THE BIBLE?
NEW TESTAMENT

The New Testament is a collection of 27 books and letters. It tells us of God's Son and Anointed One, Jesus Christ, and the wonderful salvation that He purchased for us. The books of the New Testament are grouped into 4 categories:

The Gospel and Acts

This group contains the four Gospels which are Mathew, Mark, Luke and John. The term "gospel" means "good news" and these four Gospels tell the good news about Jesus Christ. The group also contains the book of Acts which tells how the good news spread in the years after Jesus died and was raised from death.

Pauline Letters

This group is made up of Romans, 1st& 2nd Corinthians, Galatians, Ephesians, Philippians, Colossians, 1st& 2nd Thessalonians, 1st& 2nd Timothy, Titus and Philemon. These letters have traditionally been called the "Epistles" and each one is named for the group or person it was addressed too.

Other Letters

This group contains letters written by people other than Paul. It contains Hebrews, James, 1st, 2nd& 3rd John and Jude. The letter to the Hebrews doesn't give its author's name, but each of the letters is named for the person who wrote it.

Revelation

This book of Revelation is quite different from the other New Testament books, because it is a book of visions and prophecies.

ABOUT THE BOOK OF KNOWLEDGE & WISDOM

WHAT IS THE BIBLE?
PEOPLE IN THE BIBLE

Because the books of the Bible are an account or a record of God and Jesus relationship with many different people here on Earth over many thousands of years ago; here is a list of many of those individuals and the book in the Bible where you can read about them. Work with your parents to find out about them and how they met God. Jesus, or the Holy Spirit.

ACCOUNT	BOOK	ACCOUNT	BOOK
Adam and Eve	Genesis	Baby Jesus & The Wise Men	Luke
Cain and Abel	Genesis	John the Preacher baptizes Jesus	Matthew, Mark, Luke, John
Noah builds a big boat	Genesis	Satan Tempts Jesus	Matthew, Mark, Luke
Isaac	Genesis	Nicodemus visist Jesus	John
Esa and Jacob	Genesis	Woman at the well	John
Isaac	Genesis	Jesus goes fishing	Luke
Joseph and his brothers	Genesis	Man throgh the roof	Matthew, Mark, Luke
Moses	Exodus	Jesus asks Matthew for help	Matthew, Mark, Luke
Joshua	Joshua	Jesus choose 12 helpers	Mark
Gideon	Judges	Jesus preaches on a Montain	Matthew, Luke
Samson	Judges	A Boy lives again	Luke
Ruth helps Naomi	Ruth	Jesus calms the storm	Matthew, Mark, Luke
Samuel	1 Samuel	Jairus' Daughter	Matthew, Mark, Luke
The people want a king	1 Samuel	Jesus feeds 5,000	Matthew, Mark, Luke, John
David fights the giant	1 Samuel	Jesus walks on water	Matthew, Mark, John
David and Jonathan	1 Samuel	Lazarus comes alive	John
King Solomon	1 King	Ten sick men with Leprosy	Luke
God, Poor Woman & Elijah	1 King	Blind Bartimeus	Matthew, Mark, Luke
Nehemiah	Nehemiah	A woman's gift	Mark
Queen Esther	Esther	The Holy Spirit Comes	Acts
Job	Job	Saul is Jesus friend	Acts
Daniel & the lions	Daniel	Barnabaus	Acts
Jonah & the wale	Jonah	Paul in a shipwreck	Acts
Mary	Luke	A boy named Timothy	2 Timothy, Acts

ABOUT THE BOOK OF KNOWLEDGE & WISDOM

WHAT IS THE BIBLE?

What are the Ten (10) Commandments?

When Moses went up to the mountain seeking direction from God, the Lord told Moses to give the people these commandments. A commandment is an instruction that you are to follow. Just like the root word which is "command", God is telling us to follow these instructions. By following these instructions, we limit the amount of trouble you can get into because many times the trouble you are doing is associated with one of these commandments.

1. You shall have no other gods before me
2. You shall not make for youself an idol
3. You shall not misuse the name of the Lord your God
4. Remember the Sabbath day by keeping it holy
5. Honor your father and your mother

6. You shall not murder
7. You shall not commit adultery
8. You shall not steal
9. You shall not give false testimony against your neighbor.
10. You shall not covet... anything that belongs to your neighbor.

COMMANDMENT EXPLAINED

1	You won't love anything more than you love God.
2	You won't say bad things using God's name.
3	Honor the last day of the week to go to church or to honor God.
4	Respect, honor, and love your father and your mother.
5	Do not kill.
6	When you get married don't mess around with other people.
7	Don't take things that does not belong to you without asking for it.
8	Don't lie or misled people by not being honest.
9	Married people should not like their friends spouse.
10	Don't take or steal your friend's things, act greedy, or jealous.

WHY DO WE GO TO CHURCH?

ABOUT THE BOOK OF KNOWLEDGE & WISDOM

FELLOWSHIP WITH OTHER BELIEVERS

The church is a physical location where God's people come together to worship with Him like they did in the Old Testament when they would go to the Temple to experience God. When we get together with a group of people, we should be able to experience the following within our church family

A Place to Belong
God never intended for any of us to live alone or be isolated.13 Those that be planted in the house of the LORD shall flourish in the courts of our God.14 They shall still bring forth fruit in old age; they shall be fat and flourishing (KJV Psalm 92:13-14).

A Place to Connect
A place where relationships are authentic and real and you can get to know your church family, and for them to get to know you. As iron sharpens iron, a friend sharpens a friend (NLT Proverbs 27:17).

A Place to Serve
Every Christian is charged with being a part of kingdom building. Get involved in a ministry within the church where you can use your God-given gifts and talents and find enjoyment in helping and serving others. 6 Work hard, but not just to please your masters when they are watching. As slaves of Christ, do the will of God with all your heart. 7 Work with enthusiasm, as though you were working for the Lord rather than for people. (ESV Ephesians 6:6-7).

A Place to Pour
Once you've spent some time serving within a ministry, you are encouraged to share your gifts and talents to enhancing the leadership community of the church. Therefore, go and make disciples of all the nations, baptizing them in the name of the Father and the Son and the Holy Spirit. (KJV Mathew 28:19).

ABOUT THE BOOK OF KNOWLEDGE & WISDOM

WHAT IS PRAYER?

When you want to speak to your friends, your teachers, or others, we call that talking. When you want to talk to God, that is called Prayer. Because is our Heavenly Father, just like our earthly parents, He wants to have a relationship with us and for us to go to Him. Below is a list of different was to communicate to Him through Prayer. Look up the with your parents and speak with them about their meaning.

What is Prayer?

Adoration: *1 Chronicles 29:11*_____
Confession: *1 John 1:9*_____
Thanksgiving: *Ephesians 5:20*_____
Supplication: *Philippians 4:6-7*_____

Other Types of Prayers

Intercession: *1 Timothy 2:1*_____
Affirmation: *John 17:8*_____
Positive: *Psalms 34:17*_____
Listening: *Jeremiah 29:12*_____
Meditation: *Psalms 119:148*_____
Singing: *Ephesians 5:19-20*_____
Tongues: *Acts 2:4*_____

Ways to Pray

Standing: *1 Samuel 1:26*_____
Hands Raised: *1 Timothy 2:8*_____
Sitting: *2 Samuel 7:18*_____
Kneeling: *1 Kings 8:54*_____
Bowing: *Exodus 4:31*_____
Face Down Prayers: *Mathew 26:39*_____
Standing: *1 Kings 8:22-33*_____

ABOUT THE BOOK OF KNOWLEDGE & WISDOM

WHAT IS SIN?

There are many in the Bible that identify what is considered "sin" in the Lord's eye. Below is a list of some of the things we do that God considers to be a sin. But this IS NOT the complete list. But it is a great start when you are trying to understand what are the thins we do that makes God unhappy with us. Remember, there is no "perfect" person so the goal about sin is to try very hard not to do these things. Try your best to please God because when you please Him, you will make your parents and family very happy.

Everyone who sins breaks the law; in fact, sin is lawlessness (NIV 1 John 3:4.) 9 The coming of the lawless one will be in accordance with the work of Satan displayed in all kinds of counterfeit miracles, signs and wonders,10 and in every sort of evil that deceives those who are perishing. They perish because they refused to love the truth and so be saved (NIV 2 Thessalonians 2:9-10).

1 Corinthians 6:9-10; 1 Corinthians 6:13,18; 1 Corinthians 5:9-13; 1 Timothy 1:9-11; Colossians 3:5-9; Romans 1:24-32;Romans 1:28-32; Ephesians 5:3-7,11,15-18; Galatians 5:19-21; Proverbs 6:16-19; Revelation 22:15; 1 Timothy 11-15

Adulterers	Practice falsehood	Idolators	Perverts
Anger	Envy	Immorality	Rageful
Arrogant	Evil	Impurity	Rebels
Boastful	Factions	Irreligious	Ruthless
Busybodies	Faithless	Insolent	Selfish ambition
Coarse joking	False witness	Jealousy	Senseless
Cowardly	Foolish talk	Lawbreakers	Sexually immoral
Debauchery	Follow Satan	Liars	Slanderers
Deceit	Idolaters	lust	Slave traders
Debauchery	Gossips	Male prostitutes	Strife
Depravity	Greedy	Malice	Swindlers
Discord	Hatred	Murderers	Thieves
Disobedient	Heartless	Obscene language	Vile
Dissension	Homosexual offenders	Orgies	Wicked schemes
Drunkards	Idle	Perjurers	Witchcraft

KEEP, START, STOP

In my career as an application testing engineer, I work alongside developers where we design websites, databases, we are charged to ensure the design and implementation of software is sound based on the business requesting the work, and the customers who will be using the application. We use the "Agile" process and methodology to ensure the team works together to achieve our goals in an collective fashion. At the end of our designated time period, the team reflects on the implementation of our work and discuss what worked well, and what we can do to better. In your reflection of Proverbs, you will ask yourself the following questions:

KEEP DOING – If your behavior aligns with the then you should KEEP DOING whatever you're doing. It can be hard staying the course, but when you reflect over your behavior and you discover it helps you do what God desires, you feel encouraged to keep doing it.

START DOING – After reflecting on the you may find you have not begun aligning your character according to God's will and this time of reflection will give you the incentive you need to START DOING things differently so that you can.

STOP DOING – After reflecting on the scripture, you may find your "blind spot" or the behavior you exhibit that causes you to fall out of the will and the character that God desires for you to exhibit. This is the time to identify what you need to STOP DOING and think about the steps you can take to change that behavior so that you can walk in the light of God for your life.

This same process will help you learn how to discover your blind spots so at the end of each section of the book, you will have the chance to reflect on what was written in the chapter and use the pages provided to note what you will change to align your character to those seeking wisdom from the Lord.

Why Study the Book of Proverbs

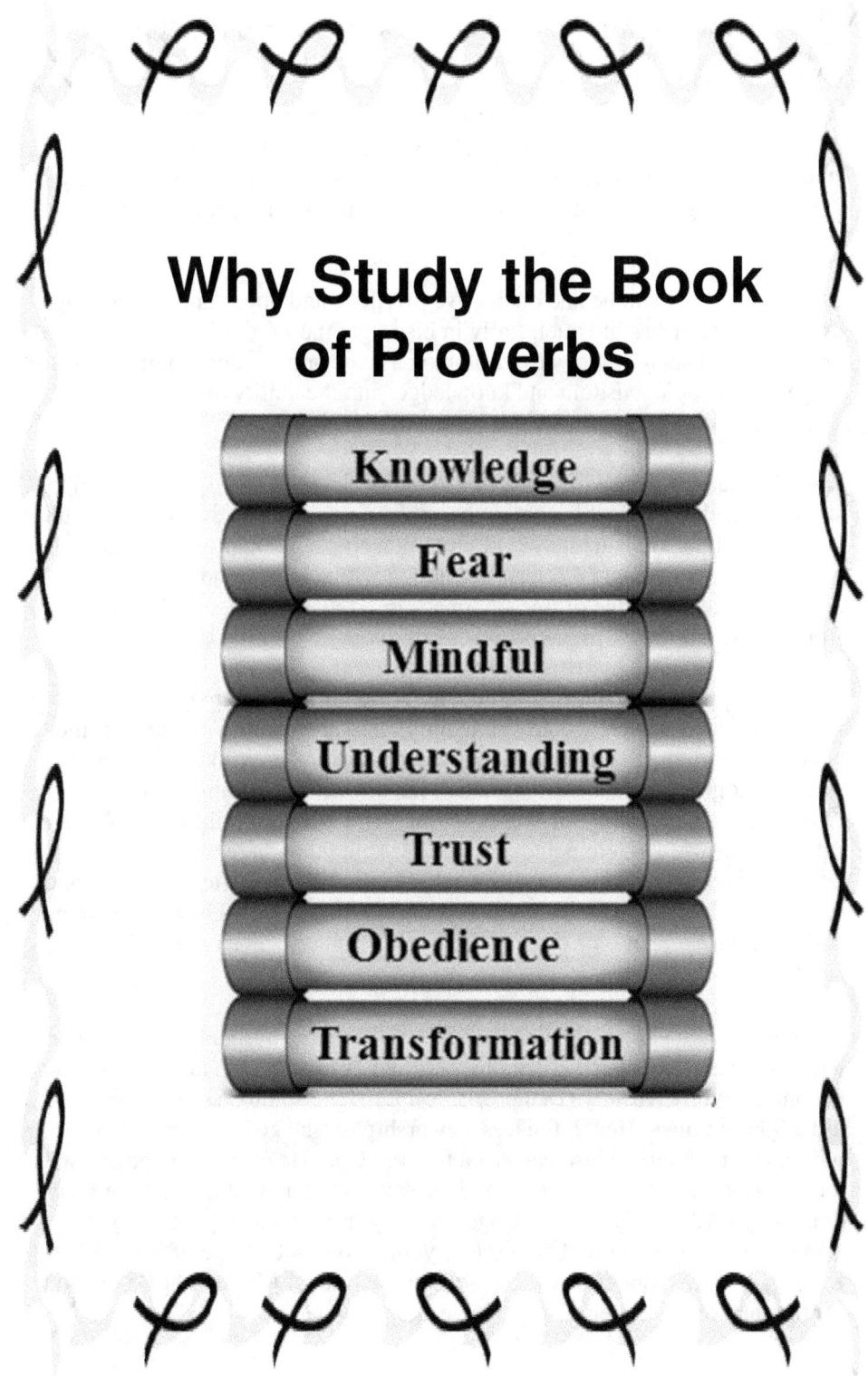

WHY STUDY THE BOOK OF PROVERBS

Acquiring wisdom and knowing how to avoid the pitfalls of folly lead to personal well-being, happy family relationships, fruitful labors and good standing in the community. Although Proverbs is a practical book dealing with the art of living, it bases its practical wisdom solidly on the fear or reverence of the Lord.

Solomon had the unique and distinctive privilege and opportunity to be king over 12 united tribes of Israel. Early in his reign, the Lord asked Solomon in a dream, "What shall I give you?" Solomon asked for an understanding heart to judge God' people, wisdom and knowledge, and the ability to discern between good and evil.

God blessed Solomon with wisdom and understanding, and exalted him in the sight of Israel. His wisdom quickly became known worldwide and his wealth exceeded all the kings in the world. Solomon spoke 3,000 proverbs, wrote 1,005 songs, the book of Ecclesiastes and the Song of Solomon. He accumulated knowledge of trees, animals, birds, fish and more. Men came from all nations to hear the wisdom of Solomon.

The Lord appeared again to Solomon, assuring him that his prayer had been heard. God said that He would abundantly bless and dwell with Israel, if they kept Him first, and that He would be with Solomon, "If you keep My statutes and My judgments, then I will establish the throne of your kingdom, as I covenanted with David your father, saying, You shall not fail to have a man as ruler in Israel." But God included a stern warning that there would be severe consequences if Solomon and the people of Israel turned away from Him and worshipped idols. "I will uproot them from My land which I have given them, and this house which I have sanctified for My name I will cast out of My sight."

Although God had forbidden marriages between Israelites and people of other nations (Deuteronomy 7:1-4) and had warned against having many wives, and becoming overly wealthy (Deuteronomy 17:17), in Solomon's latter years, he did all these things. He built places of worship for the gods of his foreign wives, and they turned his heart from the true God. He even participated in their rituals. This displeased God and He said to Solomon, "Because you have done this, I will surely tear the kingdom away from you and give it to your servant. Nevertheless I will not do it in your days, for the sake of your father David. I will give one tribe to your son for the sake of My servant David, and for the sake of Jerusalem which I have chosen."

WHY STUDY THE BOOK OF PROVERBS

The Book of Proverbs was written to give "prudence to the simple, knowledge and discretion to the young" *(NIV 1:4)*, and to make the wise even wiser.

(NIV 1:1-6) [1] The proverbs of Solomon son of David, king of Israel: [2] for gaining wisdom and instruction; for understanding words of insight; [3] for receiving instruction in prudent behavior, doing what is right and just and fair; [4] for giving prudence to those who are simple, knowledge and discretion to the young [5] let the wise listen and add to their learning, and let the discerning get guidance [6] for understanding proverbs and parables, the sayings and riddles of the wise.

THE NATURAL MAN

In the Bible, Paul spoke about three types of people: The Natural Man, The Carnal Man, and The Spiritual Man.

This is the person that has not received Christ or who has chosen not to acknowledge Jesus Christ as their Lord and Savior. The "Natural Man" or those who choose to live their lives governed by their emotions and their fleshly desires feel justified in doing whatever feels right for them and to them. [1] *"As for you, you were dead in your transgressions and sins,* [2] *You used to live just like the rest of the world, full of sin, obeying Satan, the mighty prince of the power of the air. He is the spirit at work in the hearts of those who refuse to obey God.* [3] *All of us used to live that way, following the passions and desires of our evil nature. We were born with an evil nature, and we were under God's anger just like everyone else (Ephesians 2:1-3)"*. It is difficult trying to help people who have no regard for moral principles concerning what is right or wrong, or acceptable behavior because for them **everything** is acceptable and every human being has the right to do what they choose to do; good, bad or indifferent. *"But the natural man receiveth not the things of the Spirit of God: for they are foolishness unto him: neither can he know them, because they are spiritually discerned (1 Corinthians 2:14)"*.

THE CARNAL MAN

In the Book of Galatians, Paul also tells us about the Carnal Man; *"And I, brethren, could not speak unto you as unto spiritual, but as unto carnal, even as unto babes in Christ (KJV 1 Corinthians 3:1). For ye are yet carnal: for whereas there is among you envying, and strife, and divisions, are ye not carnal, and walk as men (KJV 1 Corinthians 3:3)?"* Paul also lists the works of the flesh in his writing to the Galatians; *"Now the works of the flesh are manifest, which are these; Adultery, fornication, uncleanness, lasciviousness (KJV Galatians 5:19), idolatry, witchcraft, hatred, variance, emulations, wrath, strife, seditions, heresies (KJV Galatians 5:20), envying, murders, drunkenness, revelings, and such like: of the which I tell you before, as I have also told you in time past, that they which do such things shall not inherit the kingdom of God (KJV Galatians 5:21)"*.

In these verses, Paul states they are "babes in Christ", which mean he recognizes they accept who God is, but he knows he can't speak to them about the things of the spirit, because their actions were "carnal". The carnal man receives Jesus Christ as his Lord and Savior; yet he lives his life like he hasn't. Their behavior models that of carnality. We all know a few people who live like this. They go to church, read their Bible, and can even hold an "intelligent" conversation with other believers about faith while at the same time they live their life as though they do not know who Jesus Christ. They are carnal in their thoughts and ways thus

The Carnal Minded Christian. Today, Carnal Minded Christians always try to "justify" their actions by saying *"we know we all fall short, and that we are forgiven of our sins,"* yet as a Christian they keep forgetting that the 1st step to being saved is repenting of your sins. When we let go, but then pick up the sin and the behavior that is not becoming of a Christian, time after time, again and again, in those moments we find ourselves engaging in carnal behavior thus the label Carnal Minded Christians. This behavior is at the heart of what separates Church Folks vs Christians. Church folks know God and believe in His word, but yet they do and say what they want to. Christians are mindful of God's will for their lives and allow the Holy Spirit to convict them when their actions are contrary to God's will. That is the difference. It is not our job to judge. It is better to see church folks at least go to church, than to choose to disregard who He is. TV shows depict messages about "church folks" because it's easier to make you believe all God fearing, Bible, believers act that way. We must let our light shine so that others can see who He really is and not the Carnal depiction of Christians that non believers want people to see.

THE SPIRITUAL MAN

The word "Spiritual" deals with your health while "Maturity" deals with your growth. God wants you to grow. We are designed to grow. Spiritual Maturity is a journey that one embarks upon but is never ending. Though we may never reach a complete level of Spiritual Maturity –we should always be in a process of learning, growing, and striving to be Christ Like. Our level of spiritual maturity is also displayed through our Christ-Like behavior with everyone we come in contact with on a day to day basis. Your levels of blessings are based on your level of maturity and capabilities *(Matthew 25.15, Galatians 4.1-3),* and your level of growth is based on your desire to grow *(1 Peter 2.1).* Your spiritual growth is not based on the knowledge you have obtained, but in your works, deeds, behavior, and beliefs. I like to use the phrase "Don't Talk About It, Be About It"

What will you do, starting today to be a bold witness for the Lord in your home and in your community?

Think: WWJD in all Matters

Talk: Communicate the kingdom to everyone

Be: Living the Kingdom Life Daily

(Romans 12:2).

The 7 Principles for obtaining Wisdom from the Lord

7 PRINCIPLES FOR WISDOM

Knowledge: Once we are saved (or reborn) this is the beginning of our journey where God expects us to grow and mature as Christians. This is done through growing in God, the Holy Spirit and Jesus.

Fear: By having a deep reverence in God. For this is the first step towards having true wisdom.

Mindful: When mindful of God, You're sensitive to the Holy Spirit and your mind is set to love and obey God.

Understanding: Of God is knowledge gained by comprehending

Trust: Absolute unwavering belief.

Obedience: Willingly submit to God's authority.

Our transformation begins from the old nature that's led by the flesh (emotions, feelings, sight). To the new nature now being led by the Holy Spirit (not by emotions, feeling, faith). This is gained through **knowledge** and the teachings of God, the Holy Spirit and Jesus Christ. Having **fear** of God means to show a deep reverence for Him. For this is the first step towards having true wisdom. When we are **mindful** of God, we are sensitive to the Holy Spirit and our mind is set to love and obey God. To understand God means having the knowledge gained through the process of comprehending and **trust**ing willingly with absolute unwavering belief that we will submit to God's Authority.

7 PRINCIPLES FOR WISDOM

For the true process of Transformation is one's ability to use Wisdom for God's purpose and his glory.

Once we have been transformed, we can now walk in Spiritual Maturity and;

1) We are not constantly drawn into jealousy and strife

2) We train ourselves to discern the difference between good and evil *(Hebrews 5:14)*,

3) Actively and aggressively pursue Transformation *(Phil 3:12-15, Ephesians 4:22-24)*.

4) Have a sense of stability a) Knowing who the God is that they serve b) They are not in bondage to anyone c) Their Identity: they know who they are in Christ Jesus d) in their Emotions: they are not emotionally ruled which may cause them to react based on feeling and not on what is morally or spiritually right e) and their Speech. For they know there is power in the words they speak and so they are cautious in what they say and how it is said.

5) They are able to fulfill purpose and don't make excuses

6) Not afraid to receive correction or instruction or rebukes for their deficient understanding

7) Esteem the things of God higher than the things of this world and 8) they are able to recognize when God is at work in a situation or circumstance.

Now let's review the 7 principles of Wisdom and what the book of Proverbs has outlined as what is required in order for us to obtain Wisdom from the Lord.

7 PRINCIPLES FOR WISDOM

Knowledge of the Lord – I
What does the book of Proverbs say?

In the Beginning

(KJV 8:22 - 31) [22] The Lord possessed me in the beginning of his way, before his works of old. [23] I was set up from everlasting, from the beginning, or ever the earth was. [24] When there were no depths, I was brought forth ; when there were no fountains abounding with water. [25] Before the mountains were settled , before the hills was I brought forth : [26] While as yet he had not made the earth, nor the fields, nor the highest part of the dust of the world. [27] When he prepared the heavens, I was there: when he set a compass upon the face of the depth: [28] When he established the clouds above: when he strengthened the fountains of the deep: [29] When he gave to the sea his decree, that the waters should not pass his commandment: when he appointed the foundations of the earth: [30] Then I was by him, as one brought up with him: and I was daily his delight, rejoicing always before him; [31] Rejoicing in the habitable part of his earth; and my delights were with the sons of men.

The Lord gives wisdom. Knowledge and Understanding come from his mouth (NLT 2:6).

THE CHALLENGE

Highlight the key words or themes that stand out most to you in these scriptures.

_____

_____

_____

_____

_____

7 PRINCIPLES FOR WISDOM

Knowledge of the Lord – II
What does the book of Proverbs say?

(ERV 8:1 -21) [1] Listen, Wisdom is calling. Yes, Understanding is shouting for us. [2] Wisdom stands at the top of the hill by the road where the paths meet. [3] She is near the entrance to the city, calling from the open gates. [4] "I am calling out to all of you. I am speaking to everyone. [5] You who are ignorant, learn to be wise. You who are foolish, get some common sense. [6] Listen, I have something important to say, and I am telling you what is right. [7] My words are true, and I will not say anything that is wrong. [8] Everything I say is right; there is nothing false or crooked about it. [9] These things are clear to any intelligent person. They are right to anyone with knowledge. [10] Choose discipline over silver and knowledge over the finest gold. [11] Wisdom is better than pearls, and nothing you desire compares with her. [12] "I am Wisdom. I live with Good Judgment. I am at home with Knowledge and Planning. [13] To respect the Lord means to hate evil. I hate pride and boasting, evil lives and hurtful words. [14] I have good advice and common sense to offer. I have understanding and power. [15] With my help kings rule, and governors make good laws. [16] With my help leaders govern, and important officials make good decisions. [17] I love those who love me, and those who look for me will find me. [18] With me there are riches and honor. I have lasting wealth to give to you. [19] What I give is better than fine gold. What I produce is better than pure silver. [20] I lead people the right way— along the paths of justice. [21] I give riches to those who love me, and I fill their houses with treasures.

THE CHALLENGE

Highlight the key words or themes that stand out most to you in these scriptures.

_____

_____

_____

_____

_____

7 PRINCIPLES FOR WISDOM

Knowledge of the Lord–III
What does the book of Proverbs say?

(ERV 9:1-18) [1] Wisdom has built her house. She has carved out her seven pillars. [2] She has prepared her meat. She has mixed her wine. She has set her table. [3] She has sent out her servant girls. She calls from the highest places in the city, [4] "Whoever is gullible turn in here!" She says to a person without sense, [5] "Come, eat my bread, and drink the wine I have mixed. [6] Stop being gullible and live. Start traveling the road to understanding." [7] Whoever corrects a mocker receives abuse. Whoever warns a wicked person gets hurt. [8] Do not warn a mocker, or he will hate you. Warn a wise person, and he will love you. [9] Give advice to a wise person, and he will become even wiser. Teach a righteous person, and he will learn more. [10] The fear of the Lord is the beginning of wisdom. The knowledge of the Holy One is understanding. [11] You will live longer because of me, and years will be added to your life. [12] If you are wise, your wisdom will help you. If you mock, you alone will be held responsible. [13] The woman Stupidity is loud, gullible, and ignorant. [14] She sits at the doorway of her house. She is enthroned on the high ground of the city [15] and calls to those who pass by, those minding their own business, [16] "Whoever is gullible turn in here!" She says to a person without sense, [17] "Stolen waters are sweet, and food eaten in secret is tasty." [18] But he does not know that the souls of the dead are there, that her guests are in the depths of hell.

THE CHALLENGE

Highlight the key words or themes that stand out most to you in these scriptures.

_____

_____

_____

_____

_____

7 PRINCIPLES FOR WISDOM

Fear of the Lord - I
What does the book of Proverbs say?

The Beginning of Wisdom

The fear of the Lord is the beginning of wisdom and knowledge *(KJV 1:7, NIV 9:10)* for by me thy days shall be multiplied, and the years of thy life shall be increased *(KJV 9:11)*. The Fear of the Lord teaches a man wisdom, and humility which comes before honor *(NIV 15:33)* and respect *(CEB15:33)*. Humility and the fear of the Lord bring wealth and honor and life *(NIV 22:4)*. Fear of the Lord is a life-giving fountain; it offers escape from the snares of death *(NLT 14:27)* and he who has it will have need of nothing; no evil will come his way for *(BBE 19:23)* reverence for the Lord gives confidence and security to a man and his family *(GNT 14:26)* and makes a world safe for your children *(MSG 14:26)*. It is better to be poor and fear the Lord than to be rich and in trouble *(GNT 15:16)*. Whoever despises God's words will pay the penalty, but the one who fears God's commands will be rewarded *(GNT 13:13)*.

If thou be wise, thou shalt be wise for thyself: but if thou scornest, thou alone shalt bear it *(KJV 9:12)*. My child, fear the Lord and the king, and don't associate with rebels and *(NLT 24:21)*. For their calamity shall rise suddenly; and who knoweth the ruin of them both *(KJV 24:22)?* Don't be impressed with your own wisdom. Instead, fear the Lord and turn away from evil *(NLT 3:7)*.

THE CHALLENGE

Highlight the key words or themes that stand out most to you in these scriptures.

_____

_____

_____

_____

_____

7 PRINCIPLES FOR WISDOM

Fear of the Lord – II
What does the book of Proverbs say?

Evil

By mercy and good faith evil-doing is taken away: and by the fear of the Lord men are turned away from evil *(BBE 16:6)* and is seen in hating evil: pride, a high opinion of oneself, the evil way, and the false tongue as they are unpleasing to the Lord *(BBE 8:13)*. Those who walk with integrity fear the Lord, but those who take a crooked path despise him *(CEB 14:2)*. Don't envy sinners, but always continue to fear the Lord *(NLT 23:17)*. This will give you something to hope for that will not disappoint you *(NLT 23:18)*, the reward for humility and fear of the Lord is riches and honor and life *(NRS 22:4)*.

THE CHALLENGE

Highlight the key words or themes that stand out most to you in these scriptures.

_____

_____

_____

_____

_____

_____

_____

_____

_____

7 PRINCIPLES FOR WISDOM

Fear of the Lord– III
What does the book of Proverbs say?

The Call of Wisdom

(ESV 1:20-33) [20]Wisdom cries aloud in the street, in the markets she raises her voice; [21] at the head of the noisy streets she cries out; at the entrance of the city gates she speaks: [22] "How long, O simple ones, will you love being simple? How long will scoffers delight in their scoffing and fools hate knowledge? [23] If you turn at my reproof, behold, I will pour out my spirit to you; I will make my words known to you. [24] Because I have called and you refused to listen, have stretched out my hand and no one has heeded, [25] because you have ignored all my counsel and would have none of my reproof, [26] I also will laugh at your calamity; I will mock when terror strikes you, [27] when terror strikes you like a storm and your calamity comes like a whirlwind, when distress and anguish come upon you. [28] Then they will call upon me, but I will not answer; they will seek me diligently but will not find me. [29] Because they hated knowledge and did not choose the fear of the Lord, [30] would have none of my counsel and despised all my reproof, [31] therefore they shall eat the fruit of their way, and have their fill of their own devices. [32] For the simple are killed by their turning away, and the complacency of fools destroys them; [33] but whoever listens to me will dwell secure and will be at ease, without dread of disaster".

THE CHALLENGE

Highlight the key words or themes that stand out most to you in these scriptures.

_____

_____

_____

_____

_____

7 PRINCIPLES FOR WISDOM

Mindful of the Lord
What does the book of Proverbs say?

The name of the Lord is a strong tower; the righteous run to it and are safe *(NIV 18:10)*. A man's steps are directed by the Lord. How then can anyone understand his own way *(NIV 20:24)*? Whoever despises God's words will pay the penalty, but the one who fears God's commands will be rewarded *(GNT 13:13)*.

The Lord's eyes are everywhere, keeping watch on evil and good people *(ESV 2:8)* guarding the paths of justice and watching over the way of his saints *(CEB 15:3 BBE 20:27)*. Hell and destruction are before the Lord: how much more then the hearts of the children of men *(KJV 15:11)*? Remember the Lord in everything you do, and he will show you the right way *(GNT 3:6)*. Mark well that God doesn't miss a move you make; he's aware of every step you take *(ERV 5:21)*. A person thinks all his ways are pure, but the Lord weighs your heart *(GNT 21:2)* and motives *(GNT 16:2)*. Gold and silver are tested by fire, and a person's heart is tested by the Lord *(GNT 17:3)*. Do you see a man who is wise in his own eyes? There is more hope for a fool than for him *(ESV 26:12)*.

It is a danger to a man to say without thought, It is holy, and, after taking his oaths, to be questioning if it is necessary to keep them *(BBE 20:25)*. Give honour to the Lord with your wealth, and with the first-fruits of all your increase *(BBE 3:9)* so your store-houses will be full of grain, and your vessels overflowing with new wine *(BBE 3:10)*.

THE CHALLENGE

Highlight the key words or themes that stand out most to you in these scriptures.

_____

_____

_____

_____

7 PRINCIPLES FOR WISDOM

Understand the Lord

What does the book of Proverbs say?

My son, if you receive my words and treasure up my commandments with you *(ESV 2:1)* making your ear attentive to wisdom and inclining your heart to understanding *(ESV 2:2);* if you call out for insight and raise your voice for understanding *(ESV 2:3),* and if you seek it like silver and search for it as for hidden treasures *(ESV 2:4)* then you will understand the fear of the Lord and find the knowledge of God *(ESV 2:5).* Then you will understand righteousness and justice, as well as integrity, every good course *(CEB 2:9).* Wisdom will enter your mind, and knowledge will fill you with delight *(CEB 2:10).* Discretion shall preserve thee, understanding shall keep thee *(KJV 2:11)* but if one turns away his ear from hearing the law, even his prayer is an abomination *(ESV 28:9).*

(NIV 3:13-25) [13] Blessed is the man who finds wisdom, the man who gains understanding, [14] for she is more profitable than silver and yields better returns than gold. 15 She is more precious than rubies; nothing you desire can compare with her. [16] Long life is in her right hand; in her left hand are riches and honor. [17] Her ways are pleasant ways, and all her paths are peace. [18] She is a tree of life to those who embrace her; those who lay hold of her will be blessed. [19] By wisdom the Lord laid the earth's foundations, by understanding he set the heavens in place; [20] by his knowledge the deeps were divided, and the clouds let drop the dew. [21] My son, preserve sound judgment and discernment, do not let them out of your sight; [22] they will be life for you, an ornament to grace your neck. [23] Then you will go on your way in safety, and your foot will not stumble; [24] when you lie down, you will not be afraid; when you lie down, your sleep will be sweet. [25] Have no fear of sudden disaster or of the ruin that overtakes the wicked. However, know that the great God that formed all things both rewardeth the fool, and rewardeth transgressors *(KJV 26:10).*

THE CHALLENGE

Highlight the key words or themes that stand out most to you in these scriptures.

_____

_____

7 PRINCIPLES FOR WISDOM

Trust/Acceptance of the Lord

What does the book of Proverbs say?

I want you to put your trust in the Lord; that is why I am going to tell them to you now *(ASV 23:19)*. I have written down thirty sayings for you. They contain knowledge and good advice *(ASV 23:20)*, and will teach you what the truth really is. Then when you are sent to find it out, you will bring back the right answer *(ASV 23:21)*. My son, do not forget my teaching, but let your heart keep my commandments *(ESV 3:1)*, for length of days and years of life and peace they will add to you *(ESV 3:2)*. Let not steadfast love and faithfulness forsake you; bind them around your neck; write them on the tablet of your heart *(ESV 3:3)*. So you will find favor and good success in the sight of God and man *(ESV 3:4)*. Trust in the Lord with all your heart, and do not lean on your own understanding *(ESV 3:5)*. This will give strength to your flesh, and new life to your bones *(BBE 3:8)*. Seek his will in all you do, and he will show you which path to take *(ESV 3:6)* and whoever trusts in the Lord will prosper *(NAS 28:25)* for those who go after the Lord have knowledge of all things *(BBE 28:5)*. It is dangerous to be concerned with what others think of you, but if you trust the Lord, you are safe *(GNT 29:25)*. He that handleth a matter wisely shall find good: and whoso trusteth in the Lord, happy is he *(KJV 16:20)*. My son, give me your heart, and let your eyes take delight in my ways *(BBE 23:26)*. For length of days, and years of life, and peace, will they add to thee *(ASV 3:2)*. "Turn to me when I warn you. I will generously pour out my spirit for you. I will make my words known to you *(GW 1:23)*. Wisdom will save you from evil people, from those whose words are twisted *(NLT 2:12)*. Cherish her, and she will exalt you; if you embrace her, she will honor you *(CSB 4:8)*. These men turn from the right way to walk down dark paths *(NLT 2:13)*. They take pleasure in doing wrong, and they enjoy the twisted ways of evil *(NLT 2:14)*. Their actions are crooked, and their ways are wrong *(NLT 2:15)*. Follow the steps of good men instead, and stay on the paths of the righteous *(NLT 2:20)*. For only the godly will live in the land, and those with integrity will remain in it *(NLT 2:21)*. People are trapped by their fear of others; those who trust the Lord are secure *(CEB 29:25)* and the wicked will be removed from the land, and the treacherous will be uprooted *(NLT 2:22)*.

THE CHALLENGE

Highlight the key words or themes that stand out most to you in these scriptures.

7 PRINCIPLES FOR WISDOM

Obedience to the Lords will

What does the book of Proverbs say?

Keep God's laws and you will live longer; if you ignore them, you will die *(GNT 19:16)*. Obey the Lord, be humble, and you will get riches, honor, and a long life *(GNT 22:4)*. My child, don't reject the Lord's discipline, and don't be upset when he corrects you *(NLT 3:11)*. For the Lord corrects those he loves, just as a father corrects a child in whom he delights *(NLT 3:12)*. Happy is the man in whom is the fear of the Lord at all times; but he whose heart is hard will come into trouble *(BBE 28:14)*.

(BBE 8:32-36). [32] "Now, children, listen to me. If you follow my ways, you will be happy too *(BBE 8:32, BBE 28:14)*. [33] Listen to my teaching and be wise; don't ignore what I say. [34] Whoever waits at my door and listens for me will be blessed. [35] Those who find me find life, and the Lord will reward them. [36] But those who do not find me put their lives in danger. Whoever hates me loves death". The way of the Lord is a refuge for the blameless, but it is the ruin of those who do evil *(NIV 10:29)*. Take my instruction instead of silver, and knowledge rather than choice gold *(ESV 8:10)*. There is no wisdom nor understanding nor counsel against the Lord *(KJV 21:30)*.

THE CHALLENGE

Highlight the key words or themes that stand out most to you in these scriptures.

_____

_____

_____

_____

_____

_____

7 PRINCIPLES FOR WISDOM

THINGS TO KEEP DOING

Character Transformation Reflection: What do you need to keep doing in order to prayerfully ask God to help you accept and adopt the scriptures outlined in this chapter as a measure of your faith, trust, belief and obedience to the Lord, for yourself, and to others?

_____
_____
_____
_____
_____
_____
_____
_____
_____
_____
_____
_____
_____
_____
_____
_____
_____
_____
_____
_____

7 PRINCIPLES FOR WISDOM

THINGS TO START DOING

Character Transformation Reflection: What do you need to start doing in order to prayerfully ask God to help you accept and adopt the scriptures outlined in this chapter as a measure of your faith, trust, belief and obedience to the Lord, for yourself, and to others?

_____
_____
_____
_____
_____
_____
_____
_____
_____
_____
_____
_____
_____
_____
_____
_____
_____
_____
_____
_____
_____
_____
_____

7 PRINCIPLES FOR WISDOM

THINGS TO STOP DOING

Character Transformation Reflection: What do you need to stop doing in order to prayerfully ask God to help you accept and adopt the scriptures outlined in this chapter as a measure of your faith, trust, belief and obedience to the Lord, for yourself, and to others?

_____
_____
_____
_____
_____
_____
_____
_____
_____
_____
_____
_____
_____
_____
_____
_____
_____
_____
_____
_____

CHARACTER OF THE SPIRITUAL MAN

CHARACTER OF THE SPIRITUAL MAN

You're slow to become Angry
What does the book of Proverbs say?

A wise man keeps himself under control *(NIV 29:11)*. Insightful people restrain their anger as their glory is they ignore or overlook an offense *(CEB 19:11, HNV 25:15)*. A man who is slow to anger can calm down an argument or dispute *(NAS 15:18)* for a gentle answer quiets anger *(GNT 15:1)* and he is better than a warrior who takes over a city *(NLT 16.32)*.

THE CHALLENGE

Highlight the key words or themes that stand out most to you in these scriptures.

_____

_____

_____

_____

_____

_____

_____

_____

_____

_____

CHARACTER OF THE SPIRITUAL MAN

You Apologize/Repent
What does the book of Proverbs say?

Whoever confesses their sins and stops doing wrong will receive mercy *(ERV 28:13).*

THE CHALLENGE

Highlight the key words or themes that stand out most to you in these scriptures.

_____

_____

_____

_____

_____

_____

_____

_____

_____

_____

_____

_____

_____

_____

_____

CHARACTER OF THE SPIRITUAL MAN

You're Appreciative/Thankful
What does the book of Proverbs say?

A cheerful look and good news from someone brings joy to your heart helps you be healthy in heart *(NIV 15:30)*. How good it is to get what you want *(GNT 13:19)* and if someone corrects you after a situation occurs, you appreciate it more than flattery *(GNT 28:23)*.

THE CHALLENGE

Highlight the key words or themes that stand out most to you in these scriptures.

_____

_____

_____

_____

_____

_____

_____

_____

_____

_____

_____

_____

CHARACTER OF THE SPIRITUAL MAN

You're Calm
What does the book of Proverbs say?

A truly wise person uses few words; a person with understanding is even-tempered *(NLT17:27)*.

THE CHALLENGE

Highlight the key words or themes that stand out most to you in this scripture.

_____

_____

_____

_____

_____

_____

_____

_____

_____

_____

_____

_____

_____

_____

CHARACTER OF THE SPIRITUAL MAN

You're Caring
What does the book of Proverbs say?

Don't take advantage of the poor just because you can or take advantage of those who stand helpless in court *(GNT 23:22)* for those who gives to the poor will never be in need *(BBE 28:27)*. It is better to correct someone openly than to let him think you don't care for him at all *(GNT 27:5)*.

THE CHALLENGE

Highlight the key words or themes that stand out most to you in these scriptures.

CHARACTER OF THE SPIRITUAL MAN

You're Cautious
What does the book of Proverbs say?

The wise are cautious and avoid danger *(NLT 14:16)*. A righteous man is cautious in friendship *(NIV 12:26)*. When you take your seat at the feast with a ruler, give thought with care to what is before you *(BBE 23:1)*; and put a knife to your throat, if you have a strong desire for food *(BBE 23:2)*. Don't eat at the table of a stingy person or be greedy for the fine food he serves *(GNT 23:6, 23:3)*, he may be trying to trick you *(GNT 23:3)*.

THE CHALLENGE

Highlight the key words or themes that stand out most to you in these scriptures.

___

___

___

___

___

___

___

___

___

___

___

___

CHARACTER OF THE SPIRITUAL MAN

You're Confident
What does the book of Proverbs say?

The Lord will be your confidence and is with you to keep your foot from being snared *(NIV 3:26)*. Go forward with your head up and fix your eyes forward looking straight ahead *(CSB 4:25)* for righteous people are sure of themselves *(CSB 21:29)* knowing that God is with them because when you know what You're talking about, you have something more valuable than gold or jewels *(GNT 20:15)*. For the name of the Lord is a strong tower; the righteous run to it and are safe *(NIV 18:10)*.

THE CHALLENGE

Highlight the key words or themes that stand out most to you in these scriptures.

_____

_____

_____

_____

_____

_____

_____

_____

_____

_____

_____

CHARACTER OF THE SPIRITUAL MAN

You're Considerate
What does the book of Proverbs say?

If you find honey, eat only what you need; otherwise, you'll get sick from it and vomit *(CSB 25:16)*. Don't visit your neighbors too often; they may get tired of you and come to hate you *(GNT 25:17)*. Just as damaging as a madman shooting a deadly weapon *(NLT 26:18)* is someone who lies to a friend and then says, "I was only joking" *(NLT 26:19)*. Do not keep back good from those who have a right to it, when it is in the power of your hand to do it *(BBE 3:27)*. If your enemies are starving, feed them some bread; if they are thirsty; give them water to drink *(CEB 25:21)*. We should rescue those being taken off to death; and from those staggering to the slaughter, don't hold back *(NIRV 24:11)*.

THE CHALLENGE

Highlight the key words or themes that stand out most to you in these scriptures.

_____

_____

_____

_____

_____

_____

_____

_____

_____

CHARACTER OF THE SPIRITUAL MAN

You're Courageous
What does the book of Proverbs say?

The Godly can stand as bold as a lion *(NLT 28:1)*.

THE CHALLENGE

Highlight the key words or themes that stand out most to you in this scripture.

_____
_____
_____
_____
_____
_____
_____
_____
_____
_____
_____
_____
_____

CHARACTER OF THE SPIRITUAL MAN

You're Dependable
What does the book of Proverbs say?

To those who send him, a trustworthy messenger is like the coolness of snow on a harvest day; he refreshes the life of his masters *(CSB 25:13).*

THE CHALLENGE

Highlight the key words or themes that stand out most to you in these scriptures.

_____

_____

_____

_____

_____

_____

_____

_____

_____

_____

_____

_____

_____

_____

CHARACTER OF THE SPIRITUAL MAN

You're Diligent/Hard Worker
What does the book of Proverbs say?

You will earn the trust and respect of others if you work for good *(GNT 14:22)* and hard work will give you power you need *(GNT 12:24)* to till your land and be satisfied with the bread it produces *(KJV 12:11)* for a hard-working farmer has plenty to eat *(GNT 28:19)*. Because the person who labors, labors for himself, for his hungry mouth drives him on *(NKJV 16:26)*. From the fruit of his mouth will a man have good food in full measure, and the work of a man's hands will be rewarded *(BBE 12:14)*. Show me someone who does a good job, and I will show you someone who is better than most and worthy of the company of kings *(GNT 22:9)*. He who tends the fig tree will eat its fruit, and he who cares for his master will be honored *(NAS 27:18)*. A hard worker will get everything he want *(GNT 13:4)* because in all hard work there is profit *(BBE 14:23)*. If you work hard, you will gain the fortune you desire *(GNT 12:27)*.

THE CHALLENGE

Highlight the key words or themes that stand out most to you in these scriptures.

_____
_____
_____
_____
_____
_____
_____
_____

CHARACTER OF THE SPIRITUAL MAN

You Have Discernment
What does the book of Proverbs say?

A rich man is wise in his own eyes, but a poor man who has discernment sees through him *(CSB 28:11)*.

THE CHALLENGE

Highlight the key words or themes that stand out most to you in this scripture.

_____

_____

_____

_____

_____

_____

_____

_____

_____

_____

_____

_____

_____

CHARACTER OF THE SPIRITUAL MAN

You Receive Discipline/Correction
What does the book of Proverbs say?

For this command is a lamp, this teaching is a light, and correction and instruction are the way to life *(NIV 6:23)*. Whoever loves discipline loves knowledge *(NIV 12:1)* and if you listen to correction to improve your life, you will live among the wise *(NCV 15:31)* because those who listen to correction gain understanding *(NCV 15:32)* and if you're wise, you'll learn when you're corrected *(GNT 19:25)*. It is better to correct someone openly than to let him think you don't care for him at all *(GNT 27:5)*. By the wounds of the rod evil is taken away, and blows make clean the deepest parts of the body *(BBE 20:30)*. If you are wise, you will learn when you are corrected *(GNT 19:25)* and if someone corrects you after a situation occurs, you appreciate it more than flattery *(GNT 28:23)*.

THE CHALLENGE

Highlight the key words or themes that stand out most to you in these scriptures.

_____

_____

_____

_____

_____

_____

_____

_____

_____

CHARACTER OF THE SPIRITUAL MAN

You Show Empathy
What does the book of Proverbs say?

Do not rejoice when your enemy falls, and do not let your heart be glad when he stumbles *(NAS 24:17)*. For the Lord will be displeased with you and will turn his anger away from them *(NAS 24:18)*. We should rescue those being taken off to death; and from those staggering to the slaughter, don't hold back *(NIRV 24:11)*.

THE CHALLENGE

Highlight the key words or themes that stand out most to you in these scriptures.

_____

_____

_____

_____

_____

_____

_____

_____

_____

_____

_____

_____

CHARACTER OF THE SPIRITUAL MAN

You Encourage Others
What does the book of Proverbs say?

Worry weighs us down; a cheerful word picks us up *(MSG12:25)*.

THE CHALLENGE

Highlight the key words or themes that stand out most to you in this scripture.

_____
_____
_____
_____
_____
_____
_____
_____
_____
_____
_____
_____
_____
_____

CHARACTER OF THE SPIRITUAL MAN

You're Fair
What does the book of Proverbs say?

Showing partiality is not good, because some people will turn on you even for a piece of bread *(GW 28:21)*, being righteousness and showing justice is more acceptable to the Lord than sacrifice *(ESV 21:3)*. He protects those who treat others fairly, and guards those who are devoted to him *(GNT 2:8)*. Then you will understand righteousness and justice, as well as integrity, every good course *(CEB 2:9)*. Do not keep back good from those who have a right to it, when it is in the power of your hand to do it *(BBE 3:27)* and speak up and judge fairly; defend the rights of the poor and needy *(NIV 31:9)*. It is not good to be partial to the wicked or to deprive the innocent of justice *(NIV 18:5)*.

THE CHALLENGE

Highlight the key words or themes that stand out most to you in these scriptures.

_____

_____

_____

_____

_____

_____

_____

_____

_____

CHARACTER OF THE SPIRITUAL MAN

You're Financially Conscience - I
What does the book of Proverbs say?

Origin of Wealth

Obey the Lord, be humble *(GNT 22:4)* and wisdom offers you long life, as well as wealth and honor *(GNT 3:16, 22:4)*. Acquiring wisdom is much better than gold, and acquiring understanding is better than silver *(CEB 16:16)*. The blessing of the Lord brings wealth, and he adds no trouble to it *(NIV 10:22)*. He that maketh haste to be rich shall not be innocent *(KJV 28:20)* for selfish people are in such a hurry to get rich that they do not know when poverty is about to strike *(GNT 28:22)*. Aggressive people will get rich *(GNT 11:16)* but riches are of no help on the day of fury, but righteousness saves from death *(GW 11:4)*. The wise have wealth and luxury, but fools spend whatever they get *(NLT 21:20)*. A generous person will be made rich, and whoever satisfies others will himself be satisfied *(GW 11:25)*.

Be wise enough not to wear yourself out trying to get rich *(GNT 23:4)*. Your money can be gone in a flash, as if it had grown wings and flown away like an eagle *(GNT 23:5)*. The more easily you get your wealth, the sooner you will lose it. The harder it is to earn, the more you will have *(GNT 13:11)*. An inheritance quickly gained at the beginning will not be blessed at the end *(NIV 20:21)*. Better is the poor that walketh in his integrity, than he that is perverse in [his] ways, though he be rich *(ASV 28:6)*.

THE CHALLENGE

Highlight the key words or themes that stand out most to you in these scriptures.

_____

_____

_____

_____

_____

CHARACTER OF THE SPIRITUAL MAN

You're Financially Conscience - II
What does the book of Proverbs say?

<u>Obtaining Wealth Dishonestly</u>

Wealth you get by dishonesty will do you no good, but honesty can save your life *(GNT 10:2)*. The getting of treasures by a lying tongue is a vapor driven to and fro by them that seek death *(ASV 21:6)*. Those who become rich through high interest rates gather money for those who are generous to the poor *(CEB 28:8)*.

THE CHALLENGE

Highlight the key words or themes that stand out most to you in these scriptures.

_____

_____

_____

_____

_____

_____

_____

_____

_____

_____

CHARACTER OF THE SPIRITUAL MAN

You're Financially Conscience - III
What does the book of Proverbs say?

Securing Loans (Co-signing)

My child, have you promised to be responsible for someone else's debts *(GNT 6:1)*? Do not co-sign another person's note or put up a guarantee for someone else's loan *(NLT 22:26)*. If you can't repay, why should they be able to take your bed from you *(CEB 22:27)*? If someone puts up security for a stranger, he will suffer for it, but the one who hates such agreements is protected *(CSB 11:15)*. Only someone with no sense would promise to be responsible for someone else's debts *(GNT 17:18)*. Take the garment of one who puts up security for a stranger; hold it in pledge if he does it for a wayward woman *(NIV 20:16, 27:13)*.

THE CHALLENGE

Highlight the key words or themes that stand out most to you in these scriptures.

_____

_____

_____

_____

_____

_____

_____

_____

CHARACTER OF THE SPIRITUAL MAN

You're Financially Conscience - IV
What does the book of Proverbs say?

Borrowing Money

Poor people are slaves of the rich. Borrow money and you are the lender's slave *(GNT 22:7)*. Have you been caught by your own words, trapped by your own promises *(GNT 6:2)*? Well then, my child, you are in that person's power, but this is how to get out of it: hurry to him, and beg him to release you *(GNT 6:3)*. Don't let yourself go to sleep or even stop to rest *(GNT 6:4)*. Get out of the trap like a bird or a deer escaping from a hunter *(GNT 6:5)*.

THE CHALLENGE

Highlight the key words or themes that stand out most to you in these scriptures.

_____
_____
_____
_____
_____
_____
_____
_____
_____
_____
_____

CHARACTER OF THE SPIRITUAL MAN

You're Financially Conscience - V
What does the book of Proverbs say?

Being Wealthy vs. Being Poor

The Rich

The rich man's wealth is his strong city *(KJV 10:15)* and they imagine that their wealth protects them like high, strong walls around a city *(GNT 18:11)*. Those who depend on their wealth will fall like the leaves of autumn *(GNT 11:28)*. Wealth makes a great number of friends *(BBE 19:4)*. Every man is the special friend of him who has something to give *(BBE 19:6)*. It is trouble to be rich and in trouble *(GNT 15:16)* because the rich have to use their money to save their lives *(GNT 13:8)*. It is not good to be wealthy and dishonest *(NCV 16:8)*. When the rich answer, they are rude *(GNT 18:23)* and giving to the rich certainly leads to poverty *(GW 22:16)*. Though the rich hath many friends *(KJV 14:20)* it is better a poor man who lives with integrity than a rich man who distorts right and wrong *(CSB 28:6)* because a rich man is wise in his own eyes, but a poor man who has discernment sees through him *(CSB 28:11)*.

THE CHALLENGE

Highlight the key words or themes that stand out most to you in these scriptures.

_____

_____

_____

_____

_____

_____

CHARACTER OF THE SPIRITUAL MAN

You're Financially Conscience - VI
What does the book of Proverbs say?

Being Wealthy vs. Being Poor

The Poor

It is better to be poor and fear the Lord *(GNT 15:16)* for the righteous will prosper like the leaves of summer *(GNT 11:28)*. For the poor, every day brings trouble; for the happy heart, life is a continual feast *(NLT 15:15)*. It is better to be poor and right *(NCV 16:8)*, of a lowly spirit amongst the poor *(ASV 16:19)*, and walking in innocence *(CEB 19:1)* than to be a fool. The poor and the oppressor have this in common -- the Lord gives light to the eyes of both *(NLT 29:13)* and made them both *(NLT 22:2)*. Luxury is not appropriate for a fool- how much less for a slave to rule over princes! *(CSB 19:10)*. The destruction of the poor is their poverty *(KJV 10:15)* and oppressing the poor for profit certainly leads to poverty *(GW 22:16)*. But no one threatens the poor *(GNT 13:8)* and when they speak, they have to be polite *(GNT 18:23)*. The poor man is parted from his friend *(BBE 19:4)*, and shunned by all his relatives-- how much more do his friends avoid him! Though he pursues them with pleading, they are nowhere to be found *(NIV 19:7)*. For they are hated even of his own neighbor *(KJV 14:20)*. Yet the rich man is wise in his own eyes, but a poor man who has discernment sees through him *(CSB 28:11)*.

THE CHALLENGE

Highlight the key words or themes that stand out most to you in these scriptures.

_____

_____

_____

_____

CHARACTER OF THE SPIRITUAL MAN

You're Forgiving
What does the book of Proverbs say?

Do not let mercy and truth leave you. Fasten them around your neck. Write them on the tablet of your heart *(GW 3:3)*. Insightful people restrain their anger; their glory is to ignore an offense *(CEB 19:11)*. If you want people to like you, don't be angry by what they do, forgive them when they wrong you. Remembering wrongs can break up a friendship *(GNT 17:9)* and love overlooks the wrongs that others do *(CEB 10:12, HNV 15:15)*. If your enemies are starving, feed them some bread; if they are thirsty; give them water to drink *(CEB 25:21)*. Whoever forgives an offense seeks love *(GW 17:9)* because by doing this, you will heap burning coals on their heads, and the Lord will reward you *(CEB 25:22)*.

THE CHALLENGE

Highlight the key words or themes that stand out most to you in these scriptures.

_____

_____

_____

_____

_____

_____

_____

_____

_____

CHARACTER OF THE SPIRITUAL MAN

You're Friendly
What does the book of Proverbs say?

A man that hath friends must show himself friendly and a friend will stick closer to you than a brother *(KJV 18:24)* because a true friend loves at all times, and a brother is born just for difficult times *(CSB 17:17)*.

THE CHALLENGE

Highlight the key words or themes that stand out most to you in these scriptures.

_____

_____

_____

_____

_____

_____

_____

_____

_____

_____

_____

_____

_____

CHARACTER OF THE SPIRITUAL MAN

You're Giving/Generous
What does the book of Proverbs say?

Many try to win the favor of rulers and everyone is a friend to a man who gives gifts *(CSB 19:6)* but a generous person will be made rich, and whoever satisfies others will himself be satisfied *(GW 11:25)* because the upright man gives freely, keeping nothing back *(BBE 21:26)* and he will be blessed *(ESV 11:26)*. Those who give generously receive more *(CEB 11:24)*.

THE CHALLENGE

Highlight the key words or themes that stand out most to you in these scriptures.

_____
_____
_____
_____
_____
_____
_____
_____
_____
_____
_____
_____
_____

CHARACTER OF THE SPIRITUAL MAN

You're Helpful
What does the book of Proverbs say?

He who has pity on the poor gives to the Lord, and the Lord will give him his reward *(BBE 19:17)*. A man has joy in the answer of his mouth: and a word at the right time, how good it is *(BBE 15:23)*!. It's like gold apples in a silver setting *(CEB 25:11)*.

THE CHALLENGE

Highlight the key words or themes that stand out most to you in these scriptures.

_____
_____
_____
_____
_____
_____
_____
_____
_____
_____
_____

CHARACTER OF THE SPIRITUAL MAN

You're Honest/Truthful—I
What does the book of Proverbs say?

To Others

The Lord delights in those who tell the truth *(NIV 12:22)* for It is better to be poor but honest *(GNT 19:1)* because Righteousness protects the innocent; *(GNT 13:6)*. Truth, wisdom, learning, and good sense - these are worth paying for, but too valuable for you to sell *(GNT 23:23)*. If you are good, you are guided by honesty *(GNT 11:3)*. Honest people are safe and secure *(GNT 10:9)* as they won't have any troubles *(GNT 15:19)* because the words from their mouth is a fountain of life *(CEB 10:11)*. Be kind and honest and you will live a long life; others will respect you and treat you fairly *(GNT 21:21, 12:5)*they won't say to their neighbor, "Come back later; I'll give it tomorrow"-- when they know they have it with them *(NIV 3:28)*.It is an honor to receive an honest reply *(NLT 24:26)*.

Do not let mercy and truth leave you. Fasten them around your neck. Write them on the tablet of your heart *(GW 3:3)*. The Lord delights in men who are truthful *(NIV 12:22)*. The word of truth lasts forever *(GW 12:19)*. He who hates bribes will live *(NIV 15:27)* for an honest witness tells the truth *(NLT 12:17)* and he who gives news rightly makes things well *(BBE 13:17)*. A faithful witness does not lie *(ESV 14:5)*. A truthful witness saves lives *(ESV 14:25)* so that in this way, you may know the truth and bring an accurate report to those who sent you *(NLT 22:21)*.

THE CHALLENGE

Highlight the key words or themes that stand out most to you in these scriptures.

_____

_____

_____

_____

_____

CHARACTER OF THE SPIRITUAL MAN

You're Honest/Truthful—II
What does the book of Proverbs say?

In Business

Honest balances and scales are the Lord's; all the weights in the bag are His concern *(CSB 16:11)*. The Lord detests dishonest scales, and unequal weights and measures, but he delights in an accurate weight *(CEB 11:1, BBE 20:23, BBE 20:10)*. Also let not the old landmark be moved which your fathers have put in place *(BBE 22:28)*.

In Court

An honest witness tells the truth *(NLT 12:17)*. If they pronounce a guilty person innocent, they will be cursed and hated by everyone *(GNT 24:24)*.

THE CHALLENGE

Highlight the key words or themes that stand out most to you in these scriptures.

_____

_____

_____

_____

_____

_____

_____

_____

_____

CHARACTER OF THE SPIRITUAL MAN

You're Honorable
What does the book of Proverbs say?

Obey the Lord, be humble, and you will get riches, honor, a long life *(GNT 22:4)* wisdom and wealth *(GNT 3:16)*. Avoiding a fight is a mark of honor *(NLT 20:3)*.

THE CHALLENGE

Highlight the key words or themes that stand out most to you in these scriptures.

_____

_____

_____

_____

_____

_____

_____

_____

_____

_____

_____

_____

_____

CHARACTER OF THE SPIRITUAL MAN

You're Humble
What does the book of Proverbs say?

The fear of the Lord is wise instruction, and humility comes before respect *(CEB 15:33)*. Obey the Lord, be humble, and you will get riches, honor, and a long life *(GNT 22:4)*. Wisdom brings humility *(CEB 11:2)* and humility comes before honor *(GW 18:12)*. The Lord shows favor to those who are humble *(GNT 3:34)*. It is better to be humble with lowly people *(GW 16:19)* and be lightly esteemed and has a servant. *(GNT 12:9)*. For the person who pretends to be poor has great wealth *(GW 13:7)*. If you are humble, you will be respected *(GNT 29:23)*.

THE CHALLENGE

Highlight the key words or themes that stand out most to you in these scriptures.

_____

_____

_____

_____

_____

_____

_____

_____

_____

_____

_____

CHARACTER OF THE SPIRITUAL MAN

You Have Integrity
What does the book of Proverbs say?

Just as you can see your own face reflected in water, so your heart reflects the kind of person you are *(ERV 27:19)*. He protects those who treat others fairly, and guards those who are devoted to him *(GNT 2:8)*. Then you will understand righteousness and justice, as well as integrity, every good course *(CEB 2:9)*. For it is better to be poor yet walk in integrity *(CSB 28:6)*.

THE CHALLENGE

Highlight the key words or themes that stand out most to you in these scriptures.

_____
_____
_____
_____
_____
_____
_____
_____
_____
_____
_____
_____

CHARACTER OF THE SPIRITUAL MAN

You're Joyful
What does the book of Proverbs say?

A joyful heart brightens one's face *(CEB 15:13)*.

THE CHALLENGE

Highlight the key words or themes that stand out most to you in this scripture.

_____
_____
_____
_____
_____
_____
_____
_____
_____
_____
_____
_____
_____
_____

CHARACTER OF THE SPIRITUAL MAN

You use good Judgment
What does the book of Proverbs say?

Good insight brings favor *(CEB 13:15)*. A man that is laden with the blood of any person shall flee unto the pit; let no man stay him *(ASV 28:17)*.

<u>THE CHALLENGE</u>

Highlight the key words or themes that stand out most to you in these scriptures.

_____
_____
_____
_____
_____
_____
_____
_____
_____
_____
_____
_____
_____

CHARACTER OF THE SPIRITUAL MAN

You're Kind
What does the book of Proverbs say?

She opens her mouth with wisdom; and in her tongue is the law of kindness *(KJV 31:26)*. Those who pursue righteousness and kindness will find life, righteousness, and honor *(CEB 21:21)*. What is desirable in a man is his kindness *(NAS 19:22)*. The words of the clean-hearted are pleasing *(BBE 15:26)*. You do yourself a favor when you are kind *(GNT 11:17)* because a man has joy in the answer of his mouth: and a word at the right time, how good it is! *(BBE 15:23)*, it's like golden apples on a silver tray *(CSB 25:11)*. Kind words are good medicine *(CEB 15:4)* and a gentle answer quiets anger *(GNT 15:1)*. The upright man gives attention to the cause of the poor *(BBE 29:7)*. Happy are those who are kind to the needy and their neighbors *(CEB 14:21)*. He who has pity on the poor gives to the Lord, and the Lord will give him his reward *(BBE 19:17)* kindness shown to the poor is an act of worship to the Lord *(GNT 14:31)*.

THE CHALLENGE

Highlight the key words or themes that stand out most to you in these scriptures.

_____

_____

_____

_____

_____

_____

_____

_____

CHARACTER OF THE SPIRITUAL MAN

You're a Leader—I
What does the book of Proverbs say?

His Character

The Lord controls the mind of a king as easily as he directs the course of a stream *(GNT 21:1)*. The words of a king are like a message from God, so his decisions should be fair *(NCV 16:10)*. It is the glory of God to hide things but the glory of kings to investigate them *(GW 25:2)*. The wrath of a king is as messengers of death: but a wise man will pacify it *(KJV 16:14)*. Like a roaring lion or a charging bear is a wicked ruler over a poor people *(ESV 28:15, BBE 29:2)*. Kings detest wrongdoing, for a throne is established through righteousness *(NIV 16:12)*. A leader without understanding taxes [his people] heavily, but those who hate unjust gain will live longer *(GW 28:16)* and a king will remain in power as long as his rule is honest, just, and fair *(GNT 20:28)* because fair words are not to be looked for from a foolish man, much less are false lips in a ruler *(BBE 17:7)*. Without wise leadership, a nation falls; with many counselors, there is safety *(NLT 11:14)*. A just king gives stability to his nation, but one who demands bribes destroys it *(NLT 29:4)*. When there's no vision, the people get out of control *(CEB 29:18)*.

THE CHALLENGE

Highlight the key words or themes that stand out most to you in these scriptures.

_____
_____
_____
_____
_____
_____
_____

CHARACTER OF THE SPIRITUAL MAN

You're a Leader—II
What does the book of Proverbs say?

Judgments/Rulings

The king sits in judgment and knows evil when he sees it. *(GNT 20:8)*. Kings take pleasure in honest lips; they value a man who speaks the truth *(NIV 16:13)*. A wise king will find out who is doing wrong, and will punish him without pity *(GNT 20:26)* for the king's wrath is like the loud cry of a lion, but his approval is like dew on the grass *(BBE 19:12)* anyone who provokes him endangers himself *(CSB 20:2)*. The king who is a true judge in the cause of the poor, will be safe for ever on the seat of his power *(BBE 29:14)*. When a land transgresses, it has many rulers, but with a man of understanding and knowledge, its stability will long continue *(ESV 28:2)*. In a multitude of people is the glory of a king, but without people a prince is ruined *(ESV 14:28)*. Pamper servants from a young age, and later on there will be trouble *(CEB 29:21)*. Many seek access to the ruler, but justice comes from the Lord *(CEB 29:26)*.

THE CHALLENGE

Highlight the key words or themes that stand out most to you in these scriptures.

_____
_____
_____
_____
_____
_____
_____
_____

CHARACTER OF THE SPIRITUAL MAN

You're a Leader—III
What does the book of Proverbs say?

<u>His Advisors</u>

Do you see a person who is efficient in his work? He will serve kings *(GW 22:29)*. He will not serve unknown people. If you love purity of heart and graciousness of speech, the king will be your friend *(GNT 22:11)*. For by wise guidance thou shalt make thy war; and in the multitude of counselors there is safety *(ASV 24:6)* because without advice plans go wrong, but with many advisers they succeed *(GW 15:22)*.

A king favors a wise servant, but his anger falls on a disgraceful one *(CSB 14:35)*. If a ruler gives attention to false words, all his servants are evil-doers *(BBE 29:12)*. These are more sayings of the wise: To have respect for a person's position when judging is not good *(BBE 24:23)*. But blessings are showered on those who convict the guilty *(NLT 24:25)*.

THE CHALLENGE

Highlight the key words or themes that stand out most to you in these scriptures.

_____
_____
_____
_____
_____
_____
_____
_____

CHARACTER OF THE SPIRITUAL MAN

You're Loving
What does the book of Proverbs say?

Love covers all offenses *(CEB 10:12)*. It's Better to eat vegetables with people you love than to eat the finest meat where there is hate *(GNT 15:17)*.

__THE CHALLENGE__

Highlight the key words or themes that stand out most to you in these scriptures.

_____

_____

_____

_____

_____

_____

_____

_____

_____

_____

_____

_____

_____

CHARACTER OF THE SPIRITUAL MAN

You're Mindful
What does the book of Proverbs say?

Who can say, "I have made my heart pure; I am clean from my sin" *(ESV 20:9)?* Do not lean to the right or to the left. Walk away from evil *(GW 4:27)* because the hearing ear and the seeing eye are equally the Lord's work *(BBE 20:12)*. A sensible person sees danger and takes cover *(CSB 22:3)*. Don't speak in the ears of fools, for they will scorn your insightful words *(CEB 23:9)*. A poor man that oppresseth the poor is like a sweeping rain which leaveth no food *(KJV 28:3)*. He that blesseth his friend with a loud voice, rising early in the morning, it shall be counted a curse to him *(KJV 27:14)*. Do not exploit the poor because they are poor *(NIV 22:22)*. Great curses will be on him who gives no attention to the poor *(BBE 28:27)* or those who shut their ears to the cries of the poor for they will be ignored in their own time of need *(NLT 21:13)*. The Lord will argue their case for them and threaten the life of anyone who threatens theirs *(GNT 22:23)*. When you are full, you will refuse honey, but when you are hungry, even bitter food tastes sweet *(GNT 27:7)*. If you find honey, eat only what you need; otherwise, you'll get sick from it and vomit *(CSB 25:16)*. Don't visit your neighbors too often; they may get tired of you and come to hate you *(GNT 25:17)*. Flipping a coin ends quarrels and settles issues between powerful people *(GW 18:18)*.

THE CHALLENGE

Highlight the key words or themes that stand out most to you in these scriptures.

_____

_____

_____

_____

_____

CHARACTER OF THE SPIRITUAL MAN

You're Modest/Discrete
What does the book of Proverbs say?

My son, let not them depart from thine eyes: keep sound wisdom and discretion *(KJV 3:21)* for discretion will protect you, and understanding will guard you *(NIV 2:11)* so they may preserve discretion, and their lips may keep knowledge *(ASV 5:2)*.

THE CHALLENGE

Highlight the key words or themes that stand out most to you in these scriptures.

_____

_____

_____

_____

_____

_____

_____

_____

_____

_____

_____

_____

_____

CHARACTER OF THE SPIRITUAL MAN

You're Patient
What does the book of Proverbs say?

Patience leads to abundant understanding *(CEB 14:29)* and brings peace *(GNT 15:18)*. It's wise to be patient and show what you are like by forgiving others *(CEB 19:11)* because the discretion of a man makes him slow to anger. It is his glory to overlook an offense *(HNV 25:15)*. It is also better for a man to be patient and controls his temper than to be powerful *(NLT 16:32)*. Patient persuasion can break down the strongest resistance and can even convince rulers *(GNT 25:15)*.

THE CHALLENGE

Highlight the key words or themes that stand out most to you in these scriptures.

_____

_____

_____

_____

_____

_____

_____

_____

_____

_____

_____

CHARACTER OF THE SPIRITUAL MAN

You're Peaceful/Quiet
What does the book of Proverbs say?

Even a fool, when he holds his peace, is considered wise: and he that keeps quiet is esteemed a man of understanding *(KJV 17:28)*. A tranquil heart is life to the body *(CEB 14:30)* for those purposing peace there is joy *(BBE 12:20)*. One who openly criticizes works for peace *(GNT 10:10)* for it is better to eat a dry crust of bread with peace of mind than have a banquet in a house full of trouble *(GNT 17:1)*.

THE CHALLENGE

Highlight the key words or themes that stand out most to you in these scriptures.

_____

_____

_____

_____

_____

_____

_____

_____

_____

_____

_____

_____

CHARACTER OF THE SPIRITUAL MAN

You Persevere
What does the book of Proverbs say?

The highway of the upright is to depart from evil: He that keepeth his way preserveth his soul *(ASV 16:16)*. Hope deferred makes the heart sick, but a desire fulfilled is a tree of life *(ESV 13:12)*. The righteous may fall seven times but still get up *(CEB 24:16)*.

THE CHALLENGE

Highlight the key words or themes that stand out most to you in these scriptures.

_____
_____
_____
_____
_____
_____
_____
_____
_____
_____
_____
_____
_____

CHARACTER OF THE SPIRITUAL MAN

You're a Planner
What does the book of Proverbs say?

A thing may be put to the decision of chance, but it comes about through the Lord *(BBE 16:33)* and people may plan all kinds of things, but the Lord's will is going to be done *(GNT 19:21)*, for God directs your actions *(GNT 16:9)* and has the last word *(GNT 16:1)* so commit your work to the Lord, and your plans will succeed *(GNT 16:3)*. You can get your horses ready for battle, but it is the Lord who gives victory *(GNT 21:31)*. Without any oxen to pull the plow your barn will be empty, but with them it will be full of grain *(GNT 14:4)*. Plan carefully what you do, and whatever you do will turn out right *(GNT 4:26)*. The simple believes everything, but the prudent gives thought to his steps *(ESV 14:15)*. Plan carefully and you will have plenty; if you act too quickly, you will never have enough *(GNT 21:5)*. Enthusiasm without knowledge is no good; haste makes mistakes *(NLT 19:2)*. Get good advice and you will succeed; don't go charging into battle without a plan *(GNT 20:18)*. Plans fail for lack of counsel, but with many advisers they succeed *(NIV 15:22)*.

THE CHALLENGE

Highlight the key words or themes that stand out most to you in these scriptures.

_____

_____

_____

_____

_____

_____

_____

CHARACTER OF THE SPIRITUAL MAN

You're Positive/Cheerful
What does the book of Proverbs say?

A joyful heart is good medicine *(CSB 17:22)* and with a positive spirit, a man can endure sickness *(CSB 18:14)*.

THE CHALLENGE

Highlight the key words or themes that stand out most to you in these scriptures.

_____
_____
_____
_____
_____
_____
_____
_____
_____
_____
_____
_____
_____
_____

CHARACTER OF THE SPIRITUAL MAN

You're a Provider
What does the book of Proverbs say?

Don't build your house and establish a home until your fields are ready, and you are sure that you can earn a living *(GNT 24:27)*. A person's speaking ability provides for his stomach. His talking provides him a living *(GW 18:20)*.

THE CHALLENGE

Highlight the key words or themes that stand out most to you in these scriptures.

_____

_____

_____

_____

_____

_____

_____

_____

_____

_____

_____

_____

_____

CHARACTER OF THE SPIRITUAL MAN

You're Respectful
What does the book of Proverbs say?

You will earn the trust and respect of others if you work for good *(GNT 14:22)* and if you are humble, you will be respected *(GNT 29:23)*. Those who have no respect for the law give praise to the evil-doer; but such as keep the law are against him *(BBE 28:4)*. A good name is rather to be chosen than great riches, and loving favour rather than silver and gold *(KJV 22:1)*

THE CHALLENGE

Highlight the key words or themes that stand out most to you in these scriptures.

_____
_____
_____
_____
_____
_____
_____
_____
_____
_____
_____
_____

CHARACTER OF THE SPIRITUAL MAN

You're Righteous—I
What does the book of Proverbs say?

Righteous = Favor = Wisdom

Listen, my son, and be wise, and keep your heart on the right path *(NIV 23:19)*. For the Lord is pleased with good people *(GNT 12:2)*. He takes righteous people into his confidence *(GNT 3:32)*. He has reserved priceless wisdom for them and He is a shield for those who walk in integrity *(GW 2:7)*. For their path is as the shining light, that shineth more and more unto the perfect day *(KJV 4:18)*. Among the righteous there is favor *(KJV 14:9)*, their wisdom is a crown to the wise *(BBE 14:24)*. Whoever lives right fears the Lord *(GW 14:2)*; for Righteousness is the road to life *(GNT 12:28, 10:2)*. Righteousness and justice is more acceptable to the Lord than sacrifice *(ESV 21:3)*. The Lord's blessing is on the tent of the upright *(BBE 3:33)* for when a man's ways please the Lord, he makes even his enemies to be at peace with him *(ASV 16:7)*. The Lord is happy to hear the prayer of the righteous *(ERV 15:8, ESV 15:29)* because He loves those who try to do good *(ERV 15:9)*. He protects those who treat others fairly, and guards those who are devoted to him *(GNT 2:8)*. Then you will understand righteousness and justice, as well as integrity, every good course *(CEB 2:9)*. My son, let not them depart from thine eyes: keep sound wisdom and discretion *(KJV 3:21)*. The Lord will not allow a righteous person to starve *(GW 10:3)* however know that your riches are of no help on the day of fury, you're righteousness will save you from death *(GW 11:4)* because knowledge is stored up by those who are wise *(BBE 10:14)* and when you walk with the wise you become wise *(NLT 13:20)* and when the godly succeed, everyone is glad and a city rejoices *(NLT 28:12)*. A city becomes great when the righteous give it their blessing *(GNT 11:11)*.

THE CHALLENGE

Highlight the key words or themes that stand out most to you in these scriptures.

_____

_____

_____

CHARACTER OF THE SPIRITUAL MAN

You're Righteous—II
What does the book of Proverbs say?

Has Knowledge/ Accepts Criticism & Instruction

The tongues of wise people give good expression to knowledge *(GW 15:2)* because they say things that give you new knowledge *(ESV15:7, 16:23)*. A wise man's instruction is a fountain of life, turning people away from the snares of death *(CSB 13:14)*. The heart of him that hath understanding seeks knowledge *(ASV 15:14)*, spare his words: and is of an excellent spirit *(KJV 17:27)*. Even the prudent are crowned with knowledge *(ESV 14:18)*. The godly person gives wise advice *(NLT 10:31)* and they are also glad to be instructed *(NLT 10:8)* because when the wise are instructed, they receive knowledge *(NAS 21:11)* because they listen to advice *(NCV 12:15)* as well because they know that the righteous are saved by their knowledge *(CEB 11:9)*. These wise-hearted will be named men of good sense: and by pleasing words learning is increased *(BBE 16:21)*. A wise man has great power. A man who has knowledge increases his strength *(NIRV 24:5)*.

THE CHALLENGE

Highlight the key words or themes that stand out most to you in these scriptures.

_____

_____

_____

_____

_____

_____

_____

_____

CHARACTER OF THE SPIRITUAL MAN

You're Righteous—III
What does the book of Proverbs say?

The character of a Righteous person - A

The mouth of the righteous is a fountain of life *(ASV 10:11, 10:2)* and his lips knows how to finds favor *(NIV 10:32)*. Anyone who understands what is right keeps wisdom in view *(NIRV 17:24)* for wisdom brings humility *(CEB 11:2)*. A man is praised according to his wisdom *(NIV 12:8)*. The light of righteous people beams brightly *(GNT 13:9)* and their roots cannot be moved *(GW 12:3, 10:30)*. He who guards his soul stays far from them *(NIV 22:5)*. A prudent man foreseeth the evil, and hideth himself *(KJV 27:12)*.

The righteousness of the blameless makes a straight way for them *(NIV 11:5)*. Good people are guided by their honesty *(NLT 11:3)* and Righteousness rescues those who are honest *(GNT 11:6)*. Those who do right only wish for good *(NCV 11:23)* and loves those who do right *(GNT 11:20)*, so walk in the way of good people and stay on the paths of righteous people *(GW 2:20)* because wise conduct is a pleasure to the wise *(NLT 10:23)*. The righteous stand firm *(GNT 12:12)* and they are sure of themselves *(CSB 21:29)*. The prospect of the righteous is joy *(NIV 10:28)*. Those who are good travel a road that avoids evil; so watch where you are going - it may save your life *(GNT 16:17)*. Righteousness dignifies a nation *(CEB 14:34)*. The righteous man wisely considereth the house of the wicked *(KJV 21:12)* and the upright and just seek his soul *(KJV 29:10)*. The unjust person is disgusting to the righteous *(CEB 29:27)*.

THE CHALLENGE

Highlight the key words or themes that stand out most to you in these scriptures.

_____

_____

_____

_____

CHARACTER OF THE SPIRITUAL MAN

You're Righteous—IV
What does the book of Proverbs say?

The character of a Righteous person - B

Acting justly is a joy to the righteous *(CEB 21:15)*. Those who are wise keep things calm *(GNT 29:8)* even when insulted *(NLT 12:16)*. The innocent do what is right *(GNT 21:8)*. A righteous man is cautious in friendship *(NIV 12:26)* and they turns away from evil *(ESV 14:16)* and danger *(NLT 14:15)*. Yet they care about their animal's health *(CSB 12:10)*. If a righteous person yield to the wicked it would be like a muddied spring or a polluted well *(CSB 25:26)* but one who walks in wisdom will be safe *(CSB 28:26)*. When the wicked rise, men hide themselves: but when they perish, the righteous increase *(ERV 28:28)*.

The Righteous hate lying *(CSB 13:5)* their lips disperse knowledge *(ASV 15:7)* and they only speak the truth *(ASV 12:17)*. The heart of a righteous person carefully considers how to answer *(GW 15:28)*. If a wise man goes to court with a fool, there will be ranting and raving but no resolution *(CSB 29:9)*, but a wise person quietly holds it back his anger *(NLT 29:11)*.

THE CHALLENGE

Highlight the key words or themes that stand out most to you in these scriptures.

_____

_____

_____

_____

_____

_____

_____

CHARACTER OF THE SPIRITUAL MAN

You're Righteous—V
What does the book of Proverbs say?

The Benefits of Righteousness

Wisdom will save you from the way of evil *(GW 2:12)* and deliver you from death *(ASV 10:2)*. You have no reason to fear a sudden disaster or destruction *(ERV 3:25)* because the righteousness of innocent people makes their road smooth *(GW 11:5)*. Their lips feed many *(KJV 10:21)*, they shall have good things in possession *(KJV 28:10)* they will get what they want *(GNT 10:24)* and through mercy and truth shall be to them that devise good *(ASV 14:22)* because after a whirlwind passes by the righteous stand firm forever *(CEB 10:25)*. A man's gift maketh room for him, and bringeth him before great men *(KJV 18:16)*. Those who pursue righteousness and kindness will find life, righteousness, and honor *(CEB 21:21)*. The one who searches for what is good finds favor *(CSB 11:27)* and the fruit of a righteous person is a tree of life, wisdom *(NIV 10:31)* and a winner of souls is wise *(GW 11:30)*. If the righteous person is rewarded on earth, how much more the wicked person and the sinner! *(GW 11:31)* for nothing bad happens to righteous people *(GNT 12:21)*. The path of life leads upward for the wise to keep him from going down to the grave *(NIV 15:24)*. The evil bow down before the good, the wicked at the gates of the righteous *(HNV 14:19)*. Blessings are on the head of the righteous *(ESV 10:6)*. If you do what is right, you are certain to be rewarded *(GNT 11:18, 14:14)* with good things *(GNT 13:21)* for a man of good sense makes his way straight *(BBE 15:21)*. The righteous person is rescued and escapes from trouble *(NIV 11:8-9)*. In the steps of an evil man there is a net for him, but the upright man gets away quickly and is glad *(BBE 29:6)*. Whoever is steadfast in righteousness will live *(ESV 11:19)* and eat their fill *(CEB 13:25)*. Silver hair is a beautiful crown found in a righteous life *(GW 16:31, KJV 20:29)* and the glory of young men is their strength *(KJV 20:29)*.

THE CHALLENGE

Highlight the key words or themes that stand out most to you in these scriptures.

_____

_____

CHARACTER OF THE SPIRITUAL MAN

You're Righteous—VI
What does the book of Proverbs say?

Heritage for your descendants

The wise will have glory for their heritage *(ASV 3:35)* and the house of the righteous will stand *(ESV 12:13, GW 12:7)* and will flourish *(ESV 14:11)* and there will be a great store of wealth *(BBE 15:6)* amongst them. Their descendants will escape *(GW 11:21)* the snares of death and they will have wealth to leave to their grandchildren *(GNT 13:22)* and even in death, they will find refuge *(CEB 14:32)* because they will be remembered as a blessing *(CSB 10:7)* because their lives will be based on the basis of their integrity so their children will be blessed even after they are gone *(GW 20:7)*.

THE CHALLENGE

Highlight the key words or themes that stand out most to you in these scriptures.

_____

_____

_____

_____

_____

_____

_____

_____

_____

CHARACTER OF THE SPIRITUAL MAN

You Show Self-Control
What does the book of Proverbs say?

A wise person quietly holds it back his anger *(NLT 29:11)*.

THE CHALLENGE

Highlight the key words or themes that stand out most to you in these scriptures.

_____
_____
_____
_____
_____
_____
_____
_____
_____
_____
_____
_____
_____

CHARACTER OF THE SPIRITUAL MAN

You're Teachable/Receive Counsel-I
What does the book of Proverbs say?

Receives God's Instructions

My son, forget not my law; but let thy heart keep my commandments *(ASV 3:1)*. Let them be fixed to your fingers, and recorded in your heart *(BBE 7:3)*. Keep my rules and you will have life; let my teaching be to you as the light of your eyes *(BBE 7:1)*. Tie them on your fingers as a reminder *(NLT 7:2)*. Write them deep within your heart *(NLT 7:3)*. Love wisdom like a sister; make insight a beloved member of your family *(NLT 7:4)*. Let the wise listen to these proverbs and become even wiser. Let those with understanding receive guidance *(NLT 1:5)*. For they will give you increase of days, years of life, and peace *(CEB 3:2)*. But whoever listens to me will have security. He will be safe, with no reason to be afraid. *(CSB 1:33)* for whoever heeds instruction is on the path to life *(ESV 10:17)*. Whoever obeys instruction is happy *(CEB 29:18)* because a wise man's instruction is a fountain of life *(CSB 13:14)*. Truth, wisdom, learning, and good sense - these are worth paying for, but too valuable for you to sell *(GNT 23:23)*. If you stop listening to instruction, my son, you will stray from the words of knowledge *(CSB 19:27)*. For a house is built by wisdom and it is established by understanding *(CSB 24:3)*. Where there is knowledge, the rooms are furnished with valuable and beautiful things *(GNT 24:4)*.

THE CHALLENGE

Highlight the key words or themes that stand out most to you in these scriptures.

_____

_____

_____

_____

_____

CHARACTER OF THE SPIRITUAL MAN

You're Teachable/Receive Counsel-II
What does the book of Proverbs say?

Asks/Receives Advice

Turn your ear and hear the words of the wise; focus your mind on my knowledge *(CEB 22:17)*. It will be pleasant if you keep the words in you, if you have them ready on your lips *(CEB 22:18)*. The man whose ear is open to the teaching of life will have his place among the wise *(BBE 15:31)*. The heart of the discerning acquires knowledge, for the ears of the wise seek it out *(KJV 18:15)*. It is wiser to ask for advice *(GNT 13:10)* so he who gets wisdom loves his own soul; he who cherishes understanding prospers *(NIV 19:8)*. Listen to counsel and receive instruction so that you may be wise in later life *(CSB 19:20)*. Apply yourself to instruction and listen to words of knowledge *(CSB 23:12)*. Advice comes from the deep waters of the heart; those with understanding can draw it out *(CEB 20:5)*. My child, eat honey; it is good. And just as honey from the comb is sweet on your tongue *(GNT 24:13)*, you may be sure that wisdom is good for the soul. Get wisdom and you have a bright future *(GNT 24:14)*.

THE CHALLENGE

Highlight the key words or themes that stand out most to you in these scriptures.

_____

_____

_____

_____

_____

_____

_____

CHARACTER OF THE SPIRITUAL MAN

You're Teachable/Receive Counsel-III
What does the book of Proverbs say?

Instructing Others

Instruct the wise, and they will be even wiser. Teach the righteous, and they will learn even more *(NLT 10:7)*. Anything you say to the wise will make them wiser. Whatever you tell the righteous will add to their knowledge *(GNT 9:9, BBE 10:14)* and if you correct them, they will respect you *(GNT 9:8)* because in the lips of him that hath discernment wisdom is found *(ASV 10:13)* and knowledge comes easily to the discerning *(NIV 14:6)*. For those who listen and accept correction, they grow in understanding *(NLT 15:32)* and are honored *(NLT 13:18)* because acquiring wisdom is much better than gold, and acquiring understanding is better than silver *(CEB 16:16)*.

THE CHALLENGE

Highlight the key words or themes that stand out most to you in these scriptures.

_____
_____
_____
_____
_____
_____
_____
_____

CHARACTER OF THE SPIRITUAL MAN

You Think Before You Act
What does the book of Proverbs say?

Wise people think before they act *(NLT 13:16)* as well as give thought to their ways *(NIV 14:8)*.

THE CHALLENGE

Highlight the key words or themes that stand out most to you in these scriptures.

CHARACTER OF THE SPIRITUAL MAN

You Think Before You Speak
What does the book of Proverbs say?

The intelligent person restrains his words, and one who keeps a cool head is a man of understanding *(CSB 17:27)*. There is more hope for a stupid fool than for someone who speaks without thinking *(GNT 29:20)*. The heart of a righteous person carefully considers how to answer *(GW 15:28)* because he who speaks rashly will come to ruin *(GW 13:3)*. The one who has understanding holds their tongue *(NIV 11:12)* and a sensible person discreetly hides knowledge *(GW 12:23)*. Whoever controls his mouth protects his own life *(GW 13:3)*. The first to present his case seems right, till another comes forward and questions him *(NIV 18:17)* what a shame, what folly, to give advice before listening to the facts *(CEB 18:13)*! If you want to stay out of trouble, be careful what you say *(GNT 21:23)* because what you say can preserve life or destroy it; so you must accept the consequences of your words *(GNT 18:21)*.

THE CHALLENGE

Highlight the key words or themes that stand out most to you in these scriptures.

_____

_____

_____

_____

_____

_____

_____

_____

_____

CHARACTER OF THE SPIRITUAL MAN

You're Trusting
What does the book of Proverbs say?

You will earn the trust and respect of others if you work for good *(GNT 14:22)*.

THE CHALLENGE

Highlight the key words or themes that stand out most to you in these scriptures.

_____
_____
_____
_____
_____
_____
_____
_____
_____
_____
_____
_____
_____

CHARACTER OF THE SPIRITUAL MAN

You're Understanding
What does the book of Proverbs say?

Wisdom is supreme-so get wisdom. And whatever else you get, get understanding *(CSB 4:7)*. No wisdom, no understanding, and no counsel will prevail against the Lord. *(CSB 21:30)*. Wisdom resides in an understanding heart *(CEB 14:33)*. Good understanding wins favor *(NIV 13:15)*. It is better - much better - to have wisdom and knowledge than gold and silver. *(GNT 16:16)*. Discretion will protect you, and understanding will guard you *(NIV 2:11, 5:2)*. Understanding is a fountain of life to the one who has it *(GW 16:22)*. He who gets wisdom loves his own soul, he who cherishes understanding prospers *(NIV 19:8)* and he that shutteth his lips is esteemed a man of understanding *(KJV 17:28)*. The intelligent person restrains his words, and the one who keeps a cool head is a man of understanding *(CSB 17:27)*.

THE CHALLENGE

Highlight the key words or themes that stand out most to you in these scriptures.

_____

_____

_____

_____

_____

_____

_____

_____

CHARACTER OF THE SPIRITUAL MAN

Your Words Have The Power To Heal
What does the book of Proverbs say?

A wise man's instruction is a fountain of life, turning people away from the snares of death *(CSB 13:14)*. Those who love to talk will experience the consequences, for the tongue can nourish life *(NLT 18:21)* for wisely spoken words can heal *(GNT 12:18)*. Good people will be rewarded for what they say *(GNT 13:2)* the speech of those who do right rescues them *(CEB 12:6)*. Whoever controls his mouth protects his own life *(GW 13:3)* and the lips of the wise shall preserve them *(ASV 14:3)*. A cheerful look brings joy to the heart; good news makes for good health *(NLT15:30)*. A man has joy in the answer of his mouth: and a word at the right time, how good it is! *(BBE 15:23)*. Kind words bring life *(GNT 15:4)*, and are like honey— sweet to the soul and healthy for the body *(NLT16:24)*. A word spoken at the right time is like golden apples on a silver tray *(CSB 25:11)*. The words of a man's mouth are like deep waters and the fountain of wisdom is like a flowing stream *(BBE 18:4)*. A gentle answer will calm a person's anger *(NCV15:1)* and as cold waters to a thirsty soul, so is good news from a far country *(KJV 25:25)*.

THE CHALLENGE

Highlight the key words or themes that stand out most to you in these scriptures.

_____

_____

_____

_____

_____

_____

_____

CHARACTER OF THE SPIRITUAL MAN

Your Words Should Be Few/Not Too Many
What does the book of Proverbs say?

If you are wise and smart, you will keep quiet *(GNT 10:19, GNT 11:12)*. It is foolish to speak scornfully of others. A sensible person discreetly hides knowledge *(GNT 12:23)* and idle talk leads only to poverty *(GW 14:23)*. A truly wise person uses few words *(NLT 17:27)*.

THE CHALLENGE

Highlight the key words or themes that stand out most to you in these scriptures.

_____
_____
_____
_____
_____
_____
_____
_____
_____
_____
_____
_____
_____

CHARACTER OF THE SPIRITUAL MAN

HEALTHY EMOTIONS OF THE SPIRITUAL MAN

Adventure	Bubbly	Divine	Famous	Helpful	Kind	Pretty	Respect	Sincerity
Affluent	Bright	Dazzling	Flourish	Hold	Keen	Project	Revolutionize	Smooth
Alive	Brilliant	Donate	Freedom	Honor	Learn	Protect	Robust	Sparkling
Animated	Calm	Efficient	Full	I am willing	Light	Peace	Refinement	Spiritual
Approve	Certain	Elegance	Familiar	I choose	Loveliness	Pleasure	Rejuvenate	Support
Assertive	Charitable	Encourage	Feat	I know	Luminous	Plenty	Rely	Sustain
Astute	Cherish	Energy	Fortunate	I realize	Laugh	Polish	Renowned	Thankful
Abundant	Clean	Enthuse	Fresh	Idea	Legendary	Powerful	Resound	Thrilled
Accomplishm	Commend	Essence	Funny	Increase	Lively	Principle	Restore	Trust
Active	Comradeship	Exciting	Gather	Ingenious	Leader	Prominent	Rewarding	Together
Adjust	Connected	Explore	Genuine	Inspire	Love	Proud	Simple	Triumph
Adorable	Conviction	Exultant	Glow	Intellectual	Lucrative	Paradise	Smile	Unity
Affirmation	Care	Eager	Grace	Inventive	Master	Perfect	Soul	Upbeat
Agree	Change	Effortless	Grow	I affirm	Mend	Plenteous	Spirited	Vibrant
Alliance	Charming	Embrace	Generous	I am.	Motivate	Plethora	Spontaneous	Vision
Amaze	Clarity	Endorse	Give	I create	Maintain	Popular	Silence	Vivacious
Aptitude	Clever	Enjoy	Good	I take action	Meaningful	Prepared	Solution	Welcome
Attractive	Companionship	Enthusiastic	Graceful	Ideal	Moving	Productive	Spirit	Wholesome
Accept	Confident	Established	Grin	Incredible	Marvelous	Prosperous	Splendid	Wonderful
Achievement	Constant	Exhilarating	Genius	Innate	Meditate	Purpose	Stir	Zest
Activist	Copious	Earnest	Glad	Instantaneous	Mind-Blowing	Quest	Success	Value
Admire	Courageous	Effervescent	Gorgeous	Intelligence	Modify	Quick	Sure	Venture
Adored	Cultivate	Electrifying	Gratitude	I allow	Nature	Quiet	Synchronized	Victory
Affirmative	Cute	Encompassing	Harmony	I Can	Novel	Ready	Therapeutic	Visualize
Ally	Celebrate	Energized	Healthful	I follow	Nutritious	Refresh	Thrive	Voyage
Appreciation	Cheer	Enormous	Hearty	I trust	Nourish	Relax	Tranquil	Well
Artistic	Classy	Entirely	Holy	Imaginative	Now	Remarkable	Strong	Willing
Astounding	Closeness	Esteem	Hug	Independent	Natural	Replenish	Sunny	Wondrous
Authentic	Complete	Excited	Handsome	Innovate	Nourished	Resources	Surprise	Youthful
Beaming	Connect	Expand	Healed	Instinct	Nurture	Revere	Team	
Beautiful	Content	Exquisite	Healthy	Intuitive	Openhanded	Rich	Thorough	
Blessed	Creative	Family	Heavenly	Joy	Open	Recognize	Transform	

CHARACTER OF THE SPIRITUAL MAN

THINGS TO KEEP DOING

Character Transformation Reflection: What do you need to keep doing in order to prayerfully ask God to help you accept and adopt the scriptures outlined in this chapter as a measure of your faith, trust, belief and obedience to the Lord, for yourself, and to others?

_____
_____
_____
_____
_____
_____
_____
_____
_____
_____
_____
_____
_____
_____
_____
_____
_____
_____
_____
_____
_____

CHARACTER OF THE SPIRITUAL MAN

THINGS TO START DOING

Character Transformation Reflection: What do you need to start doing in order to prayerfully ask God to help you accept and adopt the scriptures outlined in this chapter as a measure of your faith, trust, belief and obedience to the Lord, for yourself, and to others?

_____
_____
_____
_____
_____
_____
_____
_____
_____
_____
_____
_____
_____
_____
_____
_____
_____
_____
_____
_____
_____
_____
_____

CHARACTER OF THE SPIRITUAL MAN

THINGS TO STOP DOING

Character Transformation Reflection: What do you need to stop doing in order to prayerfully ask God to help you accept and adopt the scriptures outlined in this chapter as a measure of your faith, trust, belief and obedience to the Lord, for yourself, and to others?

_____
_____
_____
_____
_____
_____
_____
_____
_____
_____
_____
_____
_____
_____
_____
_____
_____
_____
_____
_____

CHARACTER OF THE NATURAL/CARNAL MAN

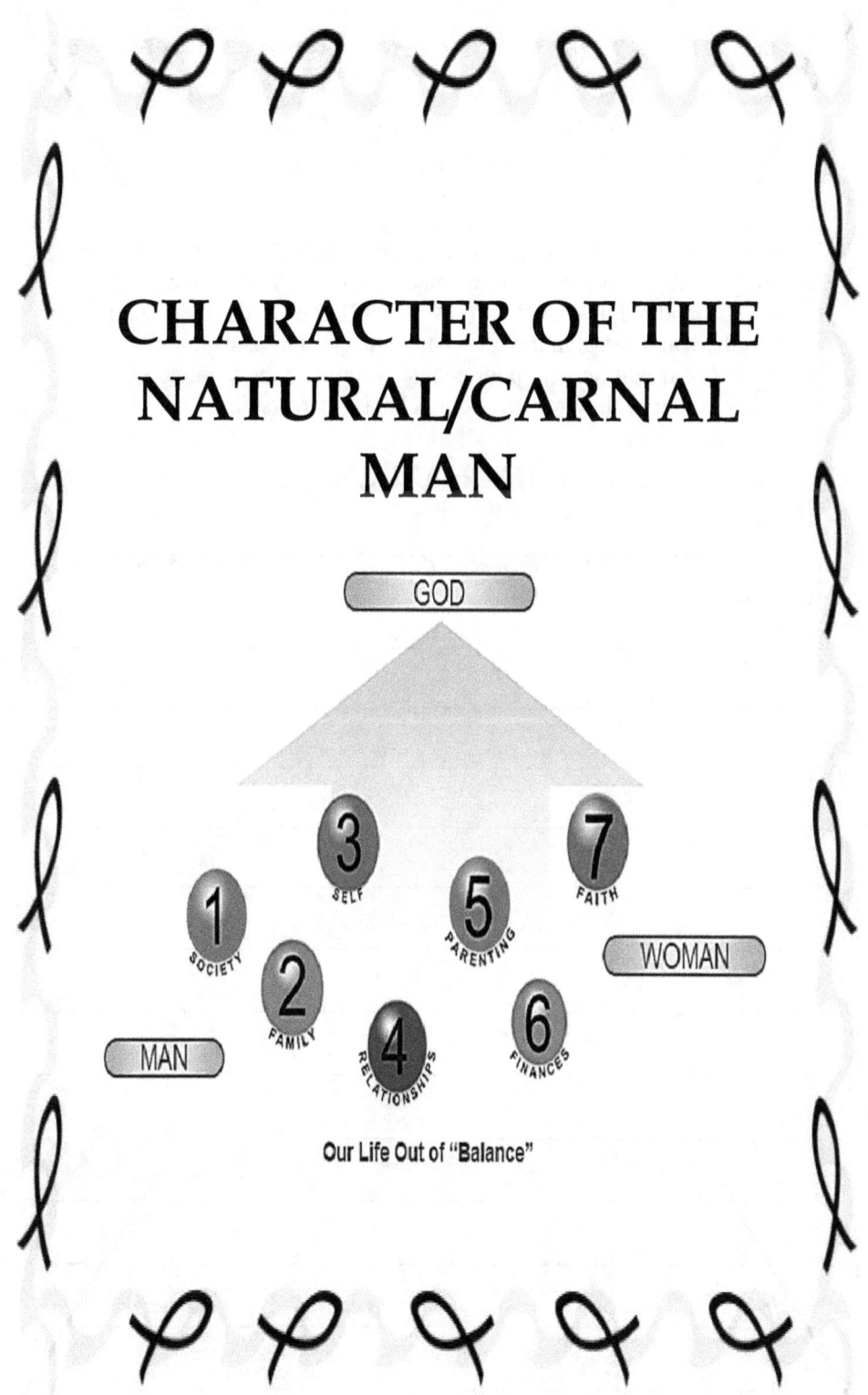

Our Life Out of "Balance"

CHARACTER OF THE NATURAL/CARNAL

You Take Advantage of People
What does the book of Proverbs say?

Do not exploit the poor because they are poor *(NIV 22:22)* and don't take advantage of the poor just because you can; and don't take advantage of those who stand helpless in court *(GNT 22:12).* The Lord will argue their case for them and threaten the life of anyone who threatens theirs *(GNT 22:23).* If you oppress poor people, you insult the God who made them; but kindness shown to the poor is an act of worship *(GNT 14:31).*

THE CHALLENGE

Highlight the key words or themes that stand out most to you in these scriptures.

_____
_____
_____
_____
_____
_____
_____
_____
_____
_____
_____
_____

CHARACTER OF THE NATURAL/CARNAL

You get Angry/Irate
What does the book of Proverbs say?

Don't befriend people controlled by anger; don't associate with hot-tempered people *(CEB 22:24)* anger is cruel and destructive, but it is nothing compared to jealousy *(GNT 27:4)*. Gossip brings anger just as surely as the north wind brings rain *(GNT 25:23)*. Fools show all their anger *(CEB 29:11)*, those who plan evil will receive trouble. For the churning of milk bringeth forth butter, and the wringing of the nose bringeth forth blood; So the forcing of wrath bringeth forth strife *(ASV 30:33)*. Their cruel anger will come to an end *(NCV 22:8)*. An unkind answer will cause more anger *(NCV15:1)*.

THE CHALLENGE

Highlight the key words or themes that stand out most to you in these scriptures.

CHARACTER OF THE NATURAL/CARNAL

You're Argumentative
What does the book of Proverbs say?

A fool's lips lead to strife, and his mouth provokes a beating *(CSB 18:6)*. Hot tempers cause arguments *(GNT 15:18)*. It's harder to make amends with an offended friend than to capture a fortified city. Arguments separate friends like a gate locked with iron bars *(NLT 18:19)*. Drive out the mocker, and out goes strife; quarrels and insults are ended *(NIV 22:10)*.

Starting a quarrel is like opening a floodgate, so stop before the argument gets out of control *(GW 17:14)*. Better to eat a dry crust of bread with peace of mind than have a banquet in a house full of trouble *(GNT 17:1)*. Only fools insist on quarreling *(NLT 20:3)*. Keep away from angry, short-tempered people *(NLT 22:24)* otherwise, you will learn their ways and become trapped *(CEB 22:25)*. If a wise man goes to court with a fool, there will be ranting and raving but no resolution *(CSB 29:9)*.

THE CHALLENGE

Highlight the key words or themes that stand out most to you in these scriptures.

_____
_____
_____
_____
_____
_____
_____
_____
_____

CHARACTER OF THE NATURAL/CARNAL

You're Arrogant/Boastful/Proud—I
What does the book of Proverbs say?

There are six things the Lord hates, seven that are detestable to him *(NIV 6:16)*, one of the six is to have haughty eyes. *(NIV 6:17)*. Mockers are proud and haughty; they act with boundless arrogance *(NLT 21:24)*. Prideful eyes, an arrogant heart, and the lamp of the wicked are all sinful *(CEB 21:4)*. The Lord detests all who are arrogant; they surely won't go unpunished *(CEB 16:5)* so people who don't know any better can learn a lesson *(GNT 19:25)* from them. The Lord will destroy the homes of arrogant men, but he will protect a widow's property *(GNT 15:25)* for He has no use for conceited people *(GNT 3:34)*.

An arrogant man stirs up strife *(CEB 28:25)* before destruction a person's heart is arrogant *(GW 18:12)*. Arrogance causes nothing but trouble *(GNT 13:10)* and pride leads to destruction, and arrogance to downfall *(GNT 16:18, 29:23)*. In the mouth of the foolish is a rod for his pride *(ASV 14:3)*. Never boast about tomorrow. You don't know what will happen between now and then *(GNT 27:1)*. It is not good to eat much honey: so for men to search their own glory is not glory *(KJV 25:6, 25:27)*. When pride comes, so does shame *(CEB 11:2)* therefore if you've been foolish and arrogant, if you've been scheming, put your hand to your mouth *(CEB 30:32)*.

THE CHALLENGE

Highlight the key words or themes that stand out most to you in these scriptures.

_____

_____

_____

_____

_____

CHARACTER OF THE NATURAL/CARNAL

You're Arrogant/Boastful/Proud—II
What does the book of Proverbs say?

Don't be impressed with your own wisdom. Instead, fear the Lord and turn away from evil *(NLT 3:7)*. Like the customer that always complains that the price is too high, but then he goes off and brags to others about the bargain he got *(GNT 20:14)*! Don't praise yourself; let others do it! *(NLT 27:2)*. To like sin is to like making trouble. If you brag all the time, you are asking for trouble *(GNT 17:19)*. Better to be humble with lowly people than to share stolen goods with arrogant people *(GW 16:19)*.

Never correct conceited people; they will hate you for it *(GNT 9:8)*. He who gives teaching to a man of pride gets shame for himself; he who says sharp words to a sinner gets a bad name *(BBE 9:7)*. Seest thou a man wise in his own conceit? There is more hope of a fool than of him *(KJV 26:12)*. A crucible is for silver and a furnace for gold, so are people in the presence of someone who praises them *(CEB 27:21)*.

THE CHALLENGE

Highlight the key words or themes that stand out most to you in these scriptures.

_____
_____
_____
_____
_____
_____
_____
_____

CHARACTER OF THE NATURAL/CARNAL

You're a Cheat
What does the book of Proverbs say?

Unequal weights, unequal measures and false scales they are all disgusting to the Lord *(BBE 20:10, 20:23)*.

THE CHALLENGE

Highlight the key words or themes that stand out most to you in these scriptures.

_____

_____

_____

_____

_____

_____

_____

_____

_____

_____

_____

_____

_____

_____

_____

CHARACTER OF THE NATURAL/CARNAL

You Lack Self-Control/Discipline
What does the book of Proverbs say?

A person without self-control is like a city with broken-down walls *(NLT 25:28).*

THE CHALLENGE

Highlight the key words or themes that stand out most to you in this scripture.

CHARACTER OF THE NATURAL/CARNAL

You Refuse Counsel/Correction
What does the book of Proverbs say?

A word of protest goes deeper into one who has sense than a hundred blows into a foolish man *(BBE 17:10)*. One who isolates himself pursues [selfish] desires; rebels against all sound judgment *(CSB 18:1)*. If you reject criticism, you only harm yourself *(NLT 15:32)*. If you do what is wrong, you will be severely punished; you will die if you do not let yourself be corrected *(GNT 15:10)*. If you ignore criticism, you will end in poverty and disgrace *(NLT 13:18)* a rod is for the back of him that is void of understanding *(ASV 10:13)*. You will groan at the end when your body and flesh are exhausted *(CEB 5:11)*. You will say "Oh, how I hated discipline! How my heart despised correction! *(GW 5:12)*. I did not give attention to the voice of my teachers, my ear was not turned to those who were guiding me *(BBE 5:13)*! I have come to the brink of utter ruin, and now I must face public disgrace." *(NAS 5:14)*.

THE CHALLENGE

Highlight the key words or themes that stand out most to you in these scriptures.

_____

_____

_____

_____

_____

_____

_____

_____

CHARACTER OF THE NATURAL/CARNAL

You Lack Direction/Motivation
What does the book of Proverbs say?

Servants cannot be corrected by mere words; though they understand, they will not respond *(NIV 29:19)*.

THE CHALLENGE

Highlight the key words or themes that stand out most to you in this scripture.

_____
_____
_____
_____
_____
_____
_____
_____
_____
_____
_____
_____
_____
_____
_____

CHARACTER OF THE NATURAL/CARNAL

You're Deceptive/Manipulative
What does the book of Proverbs say?

What you get by dishonesty you may enjoy like the finest food, but sooner or later it will be like a mouthful of sand *(GNT 20:17)*. While their hatred may be concealed by trickery, their wrongdoing will be exposed in public *(NLT 26:26)*. The wicked only want to deceive you *(GNT 12:5)*. People may cover their hatred with pleasant words, but they're deceiving you *(NLT 26:24)*. They pretend to be kind, but don't believe them. Their hearts are full of many evils *(NLT 26:25)* and a flattering mouth worketh ruin *(NLT 26:28)*. People who flatter their friends spread out a net for their feet *(CEB 29:5)*. A crucible is for silver and a furnace for gold, so are people in the presence of someone who praises them *(CEB 27:21)*. Any scheme a fool thinks up is sinful. A bribe seems magical in the eyes of those who give it, granting success to all who use it *(CEB 17:8)*.

^{13} Foolishness is that other woman, who is loud, stupid, and knows nothing. ^{14} She sits on her chair at the door of her house, up on the highest hill of the city. ^{15} When people walk by, she calls out to them. They show no interest in her, but still she says, ^{16} "Whoever needs instruction, come." She invites all the simple people and says, ^{17} "Stolen water is sweet. Stolen bread tastes good." ^{18} Those simple people don't realize that her house is full of ghosts and that her guests have entered the world of the dead *(ERV 9:13-18)*. The folly of fools is deception *(NIV 14:8)*.

THE CHALLENGE

Highlight the key words or themes that stand out most to you in these scriptures.

_____

_____

_____

_____

_____

_____

CHARACTER OF THE NATURAL/CARNAL

You're Envious/Jealous
What does the book of Proverbs say?

For jealousy is the rage of a man: therefore he will not spare in the day of vengeance *(KJV 6:34)*. Do not envy wicked or violent people *(GW 24:19, GNT 3:31)* or decide to act as they do *(GNT 3:31);* but always continue to fear the Lord *(NLT 23:17)*. Anger is cruel and destructive, but it is nothing compared to jealousy *(GNT 27:4)* for jealousy is rottenness to the bones *(CEB 14:30)*. Don't be envious of evil people and don't try to make friends with them *(GNT 24:1)*, for causing trouble is all they ever think about; every time they open their mouth someone is going to be hurt *(GNT 24:2)*. Do not get overly upset with evildoers *(GW 24:19)* because an evil person has no future, and the lamps of wicked people will be snuffed out *(GW 24:20)*.

THE CHALLENGE

Highlight the key words or themes that stand out most to you in these scriptures.

_____

_____

_____

_____

_____

_____

_____

_____

_____

_____

CHARACTER OF THE NATURAL/CARNAL

You Exaggerate
What does the book of Proverbs say?

One person pretends to be rich but has nothing. Another pretends to be poor but has great wealth *(GW13:7)*. It is better to be unimportant and have a slave than to act important and have nothing to eat *(GW 12:9)*.

THE CHALLENGE

Highlight the key words or themes that stand out most to you in these scriptures.

_____
_____
_____
_____
_____
_____
_____
_____
_____
_____
_____
_____
_____

CHARACTER OF THE NATURAL/CARNAL

You're Foolish—I
What does the book of Proverbs say?

Identifying a Foolish Person

He that hideth hatred with lying lips, and he that uttereth a slander, is a fool *(KJV 10:18, 19:1)*. People ruin their lives by their own foolishness and then are angry at the Lord *(NLT 19:3)*. The one who trusts in himself is a fool *(CSB 28:26)*. Wisdom is too high for a fool; in the assembly at the gate he has nothing to say *(NIV 24:7)*. Those who bring trouble on their families will have nothing at the end. Foolish people will always be servants to the wise *(GNT 11:29)*. What a shame, what folly, to give advice before listening to the facts! *(CEB 18:13)* but fools think they are doing right *(NCV 12:15)*, they are quick-tempered *(NLT 12:16)* and preach stupidity *(GW 12:23)*. They refuse to turn away from evil *(GNT 13:19)*. They take no pleasure in understanding, but only in expressing their opinion *(ESV 18:2)*. A fool's lips lead to strife, and his mouth provokes a beating *(CSB 18:6)* and is his devastation, and his lips are a trap for his life *(CSB 18:7)*. A scoffer loveth not to be reproved *(ASV 15:12)*. The parent of a fool has grief, and the father of a godless fool has no joy *(GW 17:21)*. Fools show all their anger *(CEB 29:11)*. As a dog goes back to its vomit, so a fool repeats his stupidity *(GW 26:11)*. Wine produces mockers; liquor leads to brawls. Whoever is led astray by drink cannot be wise *(NLT 20:1)*. Just like the legs of one who has no power of walking are hanging loose; so is a wise saying in the mouth of the foolish *(BBE 26:7)*.

THE CHALLENGE

Highlight the key words or themes that stand out most to you in these scriptures.

_____

_____

_____

_____

_____

CHARACTER OF THE NATURAL/CARNAL

You're Foolish—II
What does the book of Proverbs say?

Actions of Foolish People

Wisdom is not known in fools *(CEB 14:33)*. Like snow in summertime and rain at harvest time, so honor is not right for a fool *(GW 26:1)* and foolish behaviour is round the head of the unwise *(BBE 14:24)*. Because all the day the sinner goes after his desire *(BBE 21:26)* and the mouth of fools feedeth on folly *(ASV 15:14)*. Fair words are not to be looked for from a foolish man *(BBE 17:7)*. And don't speak in the ears of fools, for they will scorn your insightful words *(CEB 23:9)*. For the eyes of a foolish person look everywhere else *(NIRV 17:24)*. Seest thou a man wise in his own conceit? there is more hope of a fool than of him *(KJV 26:12)* for stubborn fools punish themselves with their stupidity *(GW 16:22)*. They say nothing worth hearing *(ERV 15:7)* because their mouths pour out a flood of stupidity *(GW 15:2)*. Foolish behaviour is joy to the unwise *(BBE 15:21)* and doing wrong is fun for a fool *(NLT 10:23)*. They don't think before they act and even brag about it *(NLT 13:16)*! If you let a fool deliver a message, you might as well cut off your own feet; you are asking for trouble *(GNT 26:6)*. Fools spend whatever they get *(NLT 21:20)*. A word of protest goes deeper into one who has sense than a hundred blows into a foolish man *(BBE 17:10)*. You cannot separate fools from their foolishness, even though you grind them like grain with mortar and pestle *(NLT 27:22)*. A stone is heavy, and the sand weighty; but a fool's wrath is heavier than them both *(KJV 27:3)*. As a thorn that goeth up into the hand of a drunkard, So is a parable in the mouth of fools *(ASV 26:9)*.

THE CHALLENGE

Highlight the key words or themes that stand out most to you in these scriptures.

_____

_____

_____

_____

CHARACTER OF THE NATURAL/CARNAL

You're Foolish—III
What does the book of Proverbs say?

Consequences for being Foolish

If you've been foolish and arrogant, if you've been scheming, put your hand to your mouth, *(CEB 30:32)* because people who make fun of wisdom will be punished and the backs of foolish people will be beaten *(NCV 19:29, 10:13, 26:3)*. In the mouth of the foolish is a rod for his pride; *(ASV 14:3)*. Babbling fools fall flat on their faces *(NLT 10:8)*. Shame will be the reward of the foolish *(ASV 3:35)*. Like tying a stone to a sling, so is giving honor to a fool *(GW 26:8)*. When you associate with fools you will get in trouble *(NLT 13:20)* because any fool can get himself into a quarrel *(CSB 20:3)* for the mouth of the foolish man is a destruction which is near *(BBE 10:14)* because the inexperienced keep going and are punished *(CSB 22:3)*. Fools die for want of wisdom *(KJV 10:21)*. If a wise man goes to court with a fool, there will be ranting and raving but no resolution *(CSB 29:9)*.

THE CHALLENGE

Highlight the key words or themes that stand out most to you in these scriptures.

_____

_____

_____

_____

_____

_____

_____

_____

CHARACTER OF THE NATURAL/CARNAL

You're Foolish—IV
What does the book of Proverbs say?

How to deal with a Foolish Person

Stay away from a foolish man. You won't find knowledge in what he says *(NIRV 14:7)*. The folly of fools is deception *(NIV 14:8)* and they make a mock at sin *(KJV 14:9)*. Don't answer a fool according to his foolishness, or you'll be like him yourself *(CSB 26:4)*. Give a silly answer to a silly question, and the one who asked it will realize that he's not as smart as he thinks *(GNT 26:5)*. The backslider will be fully repaid for their ways *(ESV 14:14)* because they believe anything *(ESV 14:15)*. A fool is hotheaded and yet feels secure *(ESV 14:16)* and a quick-tempered person does foolish things *(ESV 14:17)*. The simple inherit folly *(ESV 14:18)*. It is better to meet a bear robbed of her cubs than to meet a fool doing foolish things *(NCV 17:12)*. It is senseless to pay tuition to educate a fool who has no heart for wisdom *(NLT 17:16)*. Luxury is not appropriate for a fool-how much less for a slave to rule over princes! *(CSB 19:10)*. When the scoffer is punished, the naive becomes wise *(NAS 21:11)*.

THE CHALLENGE

Highlight the key words or themes that stand out most to you in these scriptures.

_____
_____
_____
_____
_____
_____

CHARACTER OF THE NATURAL/CARNAL

You Gossip/Reveal Secrets
What does the book of Proverbs say?

The words of a gossip are like tasty bits of food; people like to gobble them up *(NCV 26:22)*. Gossip is spread by wicked people; they stir up trouble and break up friendships *(GNT 16:28)* and they reveal secrets; don't associate with those who talk too much *(CEB 20:19, GW 11:13)*. A dishonest man spreads strife, and a whisperer separates close friends *(ESV 16:28)* so he that uttereth a slander, is a fool *(KJV 10:18)*. If you and your neighbor have a difference of opinion, settle it between yourselves and do not reveal any secrets *(GNT 25:9)*. Otherwise everyone will learn that you can't keep a secret, and you will never live down the shame *(GNT 25:10)*. Gossip brings just as surely as the north wind brings rain *(GNT 25:23)* and a quarrelsome person starts fights as easily as hot embers light charcoal or fire lights wood *(NLT 26:21)*. Smooth words may hide a wicked heart, just as a pretty glaze covers a clay pot *(NLT 26:23)*. A fire goes out without wood, and quarrels disappear when gossip stops *(NLT 26:20)*.

THE CHALLENGE

Highlight the key words or themes that stand out most to you in these scriptures.

_____

_____

_____

_____

_____

_____

_____

_____

CHARACTER OF THE NATURAL/CARNAL

You're Greedy/Never Satisfied
What does the book of Proverbs say?

A greedy man brings trouble to his family *(NIV 15:27)*. All day long he feels greedy *(GW 21:26)*. When you take your seat at the feast with a ruler, give thought with care to what is before you *(BBE 23:1)*; and put a knife to your throat, if you have a strong desire for food *(BBE 23:2)*. Don't eat at the table of a stingy person or be greedy for the fine food he serves *(GNT 23:6, 23:3)*, he may be trying to trick you *(GNT 23:3)* by saying "Come on and have some more," he says, but he doesn't mean it. What he thinks is what he really is *(GNT 23:7)*. You will vomit up what you have eaten, and all your flattery will be wasted *(GNT 23:8)* so don't hang out with those who get drunk on wine or those who eat too much meat *(CEB 23:20)*. Hell and destruction are never full ; so the eyes of man are never satisfied *(KJV 27:20)*.

THE CHALLENGE

Highlight the key words or themes that stand out most to you in these scriptures.

_____

_____

_____

_____

_____

_____

_____

_____

_____

_____

CHARACTER OF THE NATURAL/CARNAL

You Hold a Grudge
What does the book of Proverbs say?

Whoever keeps bringing up the issue separates the closest of friends *(GW 17:9).*

THE CHALLENGE

Highlight the key words or themes that stand out most to you in this scripture.

_____
_____
_____
_____
_____
_____
_____
_____
_____
_____
_____
_____
_____
_____

CHARACTER OF THE NATURAL/CARNAL

You're Hot/Quick Tempered
What does the book of Proverbs say?

Gossip brings anger just as surely as the north wind brings rain *(GNT 25:23)*. Fools who are quick *(NLT 12:16)* and hot tempered cause arguments *(GNT 15:18)* and people with quick tempers cause a lot of quarreling and trouble *(GNT 29:22)*. A hot-tempered man must pay the penalty; if you rescue him, you will have to do it again *(NIV 19:19)*.

THE CHALLENGE

Highlight the key words or themes that stand out most to you in these scriptures.

_____

_____

_____

_____

_____

_____

_____

_____

_____

_____

_____

_____

_____

CHARACTER OF THE NATURAL/CARNAL

You Hurt Innocent People
What does the book of Proverbs say?

There are six things the Lord hates, seven that are detestable to him: and a lying tongue, hands that shed innocent blood is one of them *(NIV 6:16).*

THE CHALLENGE

Highlight the key words or themes that stand out most to you in this scripture.

CHARACTER OF THE NATURAL/CARNAL

You're Impatient
What does the book of Proverbs say?

Impatience lead to stupid mistakes *(CEB 14:29)*.

THE CHALLENGE

Highlight the key words or themes that stand out most to you in this scripture.

_____
_____
_____
_____
_____
_____
_____
_____
_____
_____
_____
_____
_____
_____
_____

CHARACTER OF THE NATURAL/CARNAL

You Impose/You're a Meddler
What does the book of Proverbs say?

Like yanking the ears of a dog, so is one who passes by and gets involved in another person's fight *(CEB 26:17)*.

THE CHALLENGE

Highlight the key words or themes that stand out most to you in these scriptures.

_____
_____
_____
_____
_____
_____
_____
_____
_____
_____
_____
_____
_____
_____

CHARACTER OF THE NATURAL/CARNAL

You Instigate Trouble/Troublemaker/Vindictive-I
What does the book of Proverbs say?

Six things are hated by the Lord; seven things are disgusting to him *(BBE 6:16):* a mind devising wicked plans, feet that are quick to do wrong, *(GW 6:18)* and a lying witness who gives false testimony, and one who stirs up trouble among brothers *(CSB 6:19)* are three of them. A man taking false news is a cause of trouble *(BBE 13:17).* Gossip is spread by wicked people; they stir up trouble and break up friendships *(GNT 16:28).* People with no regard for others can throw whole cities into turmoil *(NLT 29:8).* Any fool can get himself into a quarrel *(CSB 20:3).* Hatred stirs up conflicts *(CSB 10:12)* but if someone looks for trouble, it will come to him *(CSB 11:27)* because trouble follows sinners everywhere *(GNT 13:21, 11:8).* Those who bring trouble on their families will have nothing at the end. Foolish people will always be servants to the wise *(GNT 11:29).*

To like sin is to like making trouble and people with quick tempers cause a lot of quarreling and trouble *(GNT 29:22)* and if you brag all the time, you are asking for trouble *(GNT 17:19).* If you let a fool deliver a message, you might as well cut off your own feet; you are asking for trouble *(GNT 26:6).* The mocker seeks wisdom and finds none *(NIV 14:6).* Evil people look for ways to harm others; even their words burn with evil *(GNT 16:27).* A dishonest man spreads strife, and a whisperer separates close friends *(ESV 16:28).* Causing trouble is all they ever think about; every time they open their mouth someone is going to be hurt *(GNT 24:2).* If you are always planning evil, you will earn a reputation as a troublemaker *(GNT 24:8).* Any scheme a fool thinks up is sinful. People hate a person who has nothing but scorn for others *(GNT 24:9).* Don't be envious of evil people, and don't try to make friends with them *(GNT 24:1).*

THE CHALLENGE

Highlight the key words or themes that stand out most to you in these scriptures.

_____

_____

_____

CHARACTER OF THE NATURAL/CARNAL

You Instigate Trouble/Troublemaker/Vindictive-II
What does the book of Proverbs say?

A rebel looks for nothing but evil. Therefore, a cruel messenger will be sent to punish him *(GW 17:11)*. Those with crooked hearts won't prosper, and those with twisted tongues will fall into trouble *(GNT 17:20)*. When the scoffer is punished, the naive becomes wise *(NAS 21:11)*. Those who plan evil will receive trouble. Their cruel anger will come to an end *(NCV 22:8)*.

My son, if sinful men entice you, do not give in to them *(NIV 1:10)*. If they say, "Come along with us; let's lie in wait for innocent blood, let's ambush some harmless soul; *(NIV 1:11)* let's swallow them alive, like the grave, and whole, like those who go down to the pit; *(NIV 1:12)* we will get all sorts of valuable things and fill our houses with plunder; *(NIV 1:13)* cast lots with us; we will all share the loot"— *(NIV 1:14)* my son, do not go along with them, do not set foot on their paths; *(NIV 1:15)* for their feet rush into evil, they are swift to shed blood. *(NIV 1:16)*. How useless to spread a net where every bird can see it! *(NIV 1:17)*. These men lie in wait for their own blood; they ambush only themselves *(NIV 1:18)*! Such are the paths of all who go after ill-gotten gain; it takes away the life of those who get it *(NIV 1:19)*.

THE CHALLENGE

Highlight the key words or themes that stand out most to you in these scriptures.

_____
_____
_____
_____
_____

CHARACTER OF THE NATURAL/CARNAL

You Instigate Trouble/Troublemaker/Vindictive-III
What does the book of Proverbs say?

It's harder to make amends with an offended friend than to capture a fortified city. Arguments separate friends like a gate locked with iron bars *(NLT 18:19)*. Do not say, "I'll do to them as they have done to me; I'll pay them back for what they did." *(NIV24:29)* and don't say, "I will get even for this wrong." Wait for the Lord to handle the matter *(NLT 20:22)*. Their hearts are corrupt and determined to do evil; they create controversies all the time *(CEB 6:14)* for this cause his downfall will be sudden; quickly he will be broken, and there will be no help for him *(BBE 6:15)*. Drive out a mocker, and conflict will leave. Quarreling and abuse will stop *(GW 22:10)*.

THE CHALLENGE

Highlight the key words or themes that stand out most to you in these scriptures.

_____

_____

_____

_____

_____

_____

_____

_____

_____

_____

CHARACTER OF THE NATURAL/CARNAL

You Get Intoxicated/Drunk
What does the book of Proverbs say?

Wine produces mockers; liquor leads to brawls. Whoever is led astray by drink cannot be wise *(NLT 20:1)*. Who has woe? Who has sorrow? Who has strife? Who has complaining? Who has wounds without cause? Who has redness of eyes *(ESV 23:29)*? It is people who drink too much wine, who try out all different kinds of strong drinks *(NCV 23:30)*. Don't look at wine when it is red, when it sparkles in the cup, going down smoothly *(CEB23:31)*. In the end, its bite is like that of a snake, its wound like the wound of a poison-snake *(BBE 23:32)*. Your eyes will see strange things, and you will say twisted things *(BBE 23:33)*. *(KJV 31:1)*. The words of king Lemuel, the prophecy that his mother taught him. What, my son? and what, the son of my womb? and what, the son of my vows? *(KJV 31:2)* Give not thy strength unto women, nor thy ways to that which destroyeth kings *(KJV 31:3)*. It is not for kings, O Lemuel, it is not for kings to drink wine; nor for princes strong drink *(KJV 31:4)*,Lest they drink , and forget the law , and pervert the judgment of any of the afflicted *(KJV 31:5)*. Give strong drink unto him that is ready to perish , and wine unto those that be of heavy hearts *(KJV 31:6)* let them drink and forget their poverty and remember their misery no more *(ESV 31:7)*. Drunkards and gluttons will be reduced to poverty. If all you do is eat and sleep, you will soon be wearing rags *(GNT 23:21)*. So don't hang out with those who get drunk on wine or those who eat too much meat *(CEB 23:20)*.

THE CHALLENGE

Highlight the key words or themes that stand out most to you in these scriptures.

_____

_____

_____

_____

_____

CHARACTER OF THE NATURAL/CARNAL

You're Judgmental
What does the book of Proverbs say?

These are more sayings of the wise: To have respect for a person's position when judging is not good *(BBE 24:23)*.

THE CHALLENGE

Highlight the key words or themes that stand out most to you in this scripture.

_____
_____
_____
_____
_____
_____
_____
_____
_____
_____
_____
_____

CHARACTER OF THE NATURAL/CARNAL

You're Lazy—I
What does the book of Proverbs say?

Take a lesson from the ants, you lazybones. Learn from their ways and be wise *(NLT 6:6)*! They have no leader, chief, or ruler *(GNT 6:7)* but they store up their food during the summer, getting ready for winter *(GNT 6:8)*. As a door turns on its hinge, so do lazy people in their beds *(CEB 26:14)*. How long will you lie there, you lazy person? When will you get up from sleeping *(NCV 6:9)*? "I'll just take a short nap," he says; "I'll fold my hands and rest a while" *(GNT 6:10)* but while he sleeps, poverty will attack him like an armed robber *(GNT 6:11)*. Being lazy will make you poor *(GNT 10:4, 20:13)*. Whoever sleeps at harvest time brings shame *(GW 10:5)*. Lazy people will never have money *(GNT 11:16)*. They will say, "There's a lion in the path! A lion in the plazas!" *(CEB 26:13)* because they refuse to work so they are only killing themselves *(GNT 21:25)*. They are as bad as someone who destroys things *(NLT 18:9)*. They will meet difficulty everywhere *(GNT 15:19)*. No matter how much a lazy person may want something, he will never get it *(GNT 13:4)*. Mere talk leads only to poverty *(NIV 14:23)* and people who waste time will always be poor *(GNT 28:19)*. Lazy people bury their hand into the bowl, too tired to return it to their mouth *(CEB 26:15)*. Lazy people think they are wiser than seven people who answer sensibly *(CEB 26:16)*. Never get a lazy person to do something for you; he will be as irritating as vinegar on your teeth or smoke in your eyes *(GNT 10:26)*. Drunkards and gluttons will be reduced to poverty. If all you do is eat and sleep, you will soon be wearing rags *(GNT 23:21)*.

THE CHALLENGE

Highlight the key words or themes that stand out most to you in these scriptures.

_____

_____

_____

_____

_____

CHARACTER OF THE NATURAL/CARNAL

You're Lazy—II
What does the book of Proverbs say?

I went by the field of the slothful, and by the vineyard of the man void of understanding *(KJV 24:30)* and it was all full of thorns, and covered with waste plants, and its stone wall was broken down. *(BBE 24:31)*. I looked at this, thought about it, and learned a lesson from it *(GNT 24:32):* a little sleep, a little rest, a little folding of the hands in sleep *(BBE 24:33)* so loss will come on you like an outlaw, and your need like an armed man *(BBE 24:34).* The sluggard does not plow after the autumn, so he begs during the harvest and has nothing *(NAS 20:4)*. The lazy do not roast their game *(NRS 12:27)*. Being lazy will make you a slave *(GNT 12:24)*. So go ahead and be lazy; sleep on, but you will go hungry *(GNT 19:15)*. Some people are too lazy to put food in their own mouths *(GNT 19:24)*.

THE CHALLENGE

Highlight the key words or themes that stand out most to you in these scriptures.

_____
_____
_____
_____
_____
_____
_____
_____
_____

CHARACTER OF THE NATURAL/CARNAL

You're a Liar
What does the book of Proverbs say?

There are six things the Lord hates, seven that are detestable to him *(NIV 6:16)* and a lying tongue *(NIV 6:17, 12:22)* and a false witness, breathing out untrue words *(BBE 6:19)* is another one.

Don't let your mouth speak dishonestly, and don't let your lips talk deviously *(CSB 4:24)*. Worthless, wicked people go around telling lies *(GNT 6:12)* signaling their true intentions to their friends by making signs with their eyes and feet and fingers *(NLT 6:13)*. Evil people listen to evil ideas, and liars listen to lies *(GNT 17:4)*. The words of a talebearer are as wounds, and they go down into the innermost parts of the belly *(KJV 18:8)*; whoever lives dishonestly will be found out *(GW 10:9)*. A lying tongue hates its victims *(NLT 26:28)* and someone who holds back the truth causes trouble *(GNT 10:10)* and a man taking false news is also a cause of trouble *(BBE 13:17)*. He that hideth hatred with lying lips, and he that uttereth a slander, is a fool *(KJV 10:18)*. People who can't be trusted are destroyed by their own dishonesty *(GNT 11:3)*. The advice of the wicked is treacherous *(NLT 12:5)* a false witness tells lies *(NLT 12:17, ESV 14:5)* and is deceitful *(ESV 14:25)* he will not go unpunished, nor will a liar escape *(NLT 19:5)* they will perish; whoever listens to him will be destroyed forever *(NLT 19:9, NIV 21:28)* but, the wicked act disgustingly and disgracefully *(CSB 13:5)*. It is a disgrace to be greedy; poor people are better off than liars *(GNT 19:22)* for it is better to be poor and walk in innocence than to have dishonest lips and be a fool *(CEB 19:1)*. Do not testify spitefully against innocent neighbors; don't lie about them *(NLT 24:28)*. A lying witness will perish *(CSB 21:28)* because lies last only a moment *(GW 12:19)*.

THE CHALLENGE

Highlight the key words or themes that stand out most to you in these scriptures.

_____

_____

_____

_____

CHARACTER OF THE NATURAL/CARNAL

You Break Laws
What does the book of Proverbs say?

Those who have no respect for the law give praise to the evil-doer; but such as keep the law are against him *(BBE 28:4).*

THE CHALLENGE

Highlight the key words or themes that stand out most to you in these scriptures.

CHARACTER OF THE NATURAL/CARNAL

You're Mean/Hateful
What does the book of Proverbs say?

The poor and the oppressor have this in common -- the Lord gives light to the eyes of both *(NLT 29:13)* but do not exploit the poor because they are poor and do not crush the needy in court *(NIV 22:22)*. The Lord will argue their case for them and threaten the life of anyone who threatens theirs *(GNT 22:23)*. If you oppress poor people, you insult the God who made them *(GNT 14:31)* and you will be punished if you take pleasure in someone's misfortune *(GNT 17:5)*. If you are cruel, you only hurt yourself *(GNT 11:17)* because deceitful words can really hurt *(CEB 15:4)*. The mocker seeks wisdom and finds none *(NIV 14:6)* don't eat the finest meat where there is hate *(GNT 15:17)*. People hate a person who has nothing but scorn for others *(GNT 24:9)*.

To impose a fine on a righteous man is not good, nor to strike the noble for their uprightness *(ESV 17:26)*. The bloodthirsty hate the upright *(KJV 29:10)*. Whoever is filled with hate disguises it with his speech, but inside he holds on to deceit *(GW 26:24)*. Keep away from angry, short-tempered people *(NLT 22:24)*. Hate stirs up conflict *(CEB 10:12)*. Those who are deceitful are hungry for violence *(GNT 13:2)*. For the churning of milk bringeth forth butter, and the wringing of the nose bringeth forth blood; So the forcing of wrath bringeth forth strife *(ASV 30:33)*. A lying tongue hates its victims *(NLT 26:28, 9:8)*. Those who despise their neighbors are sinners and *(CEB 14:21)*. Don't visit your neighbors too often; they may get tired of you and come to hate you *(GNT 25:17)*. While their hatred may be concealed by trickery, their wrongdoing will be exposed in public *(NLT 26:26)*.

THE CHALLENGE

Highlight the key words or themes that stand out most to you in these scriptures.

_____

_____

_____

_____

CHARACTER OF THE NATURAL/CARNAL

You're Promiscuous/A Loose Woman—I
What does the book of Proverbs say?

Wisdom will save you from the immoral woman, from the seductive words of the promiscuous woman *(NLT 2:16)*. She has abandoned her husband and ignores the covenant she made before God *(NLT 2:17)*. Entering her house leads to death; it is the road to the grave *(NLT 2:18)*. The man who visits her is doomed. He will never reach the paths of life *(NLT 2:19)*. He who goes in the company of loose women is a waster of wealth *(BBE 29:3)*. For a loose woman is a deep hollow, and a strange woman is a narrow water-hole *(CEB 23:27)*. Yes, she is waiting secretly like a beast for its food, and deceit by her is increased among men *(CEB 23:28)*. A continual dropping in a very rainy day and a contentious woman are a like *(KJV 27:15)*, whosoever hideth her hideth the wind, and the ointment of his right hand, which bewrayeth itself *(KJV 27:16)*.

THE CHALLENGE

Highlight the key words or themes that stand out most to you in these scriptures.

_____
_____
_____
_____
_____
_____
_____
_____
_____
_____

CHARACTER OF THE NATURAL/CARNAL

You're Promiscuous/A Loose Woman—II
What does the book of Proverbs say?

My son, remember my words. Don't forget what I have told you. ² Consider my teaching as precious as your own eyes. Obey my commands, and you will have a good life. ³ Tie them around your finger. Write them on your heart. ⁴ Treat wisdom like the woman you love and knowledge like the one dearest to you. ⁵ Wisdom will save you from that other woman, the other man's wife, who tempts you with such sweet words. ⁶ One day I was looking out my window ⁷ at some foolish teenagers and noticed one who had no sense at all. ⁸ He was walking through the marketplace and came to the corner where a certain woman lived. He then turned up the road that goes by her house. ⁹ The day was ending. The sun had set, and it was almost dark. ¹⁰ Suddenly, there she was in front of him, dressed like a prostitute. She had plans for him. ¹¹ She was a wild and rebellious woman who would not stay at home. ¹² She walked the streets, always looking for someone to trap. ¹³ She grabbed the young man and kissed him. Without shame, she looked him in the eye and said, ¹⁴ "I offered a fellowship offering today. I gave what I promised to give, ¹⁵ and I still have plenty of food left. So I came out to find you, and here You're! ¹⁶ I have clean sheets on my bed—special ones from Egypt. ¹⁷ My bed smells wonderful with myrrh, aloes, and cinnamon. ¹⁸ Come, let's enjoy ourselves all night. We can make love until dawn. ¹⁹ My husband has gone on a business trip. ²⁰ He took enough money for a long trip and won't be home for two weeks.[a]" ²¹ This is what the woman said to tempt the young man, and her smooth words tricked him. ²² He followed her, like a bull being led to the slaughter. He was like a deer walking into a trap, ²³ where a hunter waits to shoot an arrow through its heart. The boy was like a bird flying into a net, never seeing the danger he was in. ²⁴ Now, sons, listen to me. Pay attention to what I say. ²⁵ Don't let your heart lead you to an evil woman like that. Don't go where she wants to lead you. ²⁶ She has brought down some of the most powerful men; she has left many dead bodies in her path. ²⁷ Her house is the place of death. The road to it leads straight to the grave *(ERV 7:1-27).*

THE CHALLENGE

Highlight the key words or themes that stand out most to you in these scriptures.

_____

_____

CHARACTER OF THE NATURAL/CARNAL

You're Rude
What does the book of Proverbs say?

He who says sharp words to a sinner gets a bad name *(BBE 9:7)*.

THE CHALLENGE

Highlight the key words or themes that stand out most to you in this scripture.

_____
_____
_____
_____
_____
_____
_____
_____
_____
_____
_____
_____
_____
_____
_____
_____

CHARACTER OF THE NATURAL/CARNAL

You're Selfish/Stingy
What does the book of Proverbs say?

The people curse him who holds back grain, but a blessing is on the head of him who sells it *(ESV 11:26)* and don't eat at the table of a stingy person or be greedy for the fine food he serves *(GNT 23:6)*. Selfish people are in such a hurry to get rich that they do not know when poverty is about to strike *(GNT 28:22)*. Great curses will be on him who gives no attention to the poor *(BBE 28:27)* for those who are stingy with what is appropriate will grow needy *(CEB 11:24)*.

THE CHALLENGE

Highlight the key words or themes that stand out most to you in these scriptures.

_____
_____
_____
_____
_____
_____
_____
_____
_____
_____
_____

CHARACTER OF THE NATURAL/CARNAL

You're Spiteful
What does the book of Proverbs say?

Whoever hides their sins will not be successful *(ERV 28:13)*. A curse given for no reason is like a wandering bird or a flying sparrow. It doesn't go anywhere *(NIRV 26:2)*.

THE CHALLENGE

Highlight the key words or themes that stand out most to you in these scriptures.

CHARACTER OF THE NATURAL/CARNAL

You're Stubborn
What does the book of Proverbs say?

There is a way that seems right to a man, but its end is the way to death *(CSB 14:12, 16:25)*. Even in laughter a heart may be sad, and joy may end in grief *(CSB 14:13)*. If you ignore criticism, you will end in poverty and disgrace *(NLT 13:18)*. If you reject criticism, you only harm yourself *(NLT 15:32)*. One who stays stubborn after many corrections will be suddenly broken, beyond healing *(CEB 29:1)*. If you do what is wrong, you will be severely punished; you will die if you do not let yourself be corrected *(GNT 15:10)*.

THE CHALLENGE

Highlight the key words or themes that stand out most to you in these scriptures.

_____

_____

_____

_____

_____

_____

_____

_____

_____

_____

_____

CHARACTER OF THE NATURAL/CARNAL

You're a Thief
What does the book of Proverbs say?

People don't despise a thief if he steals food when he is hungry *(GNT 6:30)*, but if he is taken in the act he will have to give back seven times as much, giving up all his property which is in his house *(BBE 6:31)*. Those who share plunder with thieves hate themselves; even under oath, they don't testify *(CEB 29:24)*.

Let not the old landmark be moved which your fathers have put in place *(BBE 22:28)* and don't encroach on the fields of the fatherless *(CSB 23:10)*. God, their defender, is strong; he will take their side against you *(NCV 23:11)*.

THE CHALLENGE

Highlight the key words or themes that stand out most to you in these scriptures.

_____

_____

_____

_____

_____

_____

_____

_____

_____

_____

CHARACTER OF THE NATURAL/CARNAL

You can't be Trusted
What does the book of Proverbs say?

Don't let your mouth speak dishonestly, and don't let your lips talk deviously *(CSB 4:24)*. Those who can't be trusted are trapped by their own greed *(GNT 11:6)* and whoever lives dishonestly will be found out *(GW 10:9)*. Unreliable messengers cause trouble *(GW 13:17)*. Confidence in an unfaithful man in time of trouble is like a broken tooth, and a foot out of joint *(KJV 25:19)*.

THE CHALLENGE

Highlight the key words or themes that stand out most to you in these scriptures.

_____
_____
_____
_____
_____
_____
_____
_____
_____
_____
_____
_____
_____

CHARACTER OF THE NATURAL/CARNAL

You're Violent
What does the book of Proverbs say?

A violent man enticeth his neighbour, and leadeth him into the way that is not good *(KJV 16:29)*.

THE CHALLENGE

Highlight the key words or themes that stand out most to you in this scripture.

_____

_____

_____

_____

_____

_____

_____

_____

_____

_____

_____

_____

_____

CHARACTER OF THE NATURAL/CARNAL

You're Weak
What does the book of Proverbs say?

If you give up when trouble comes, it shows that you are weak *(NCV 24:10)*. He that followeth vain persons is void of understanding *(KJV 12:11)* and good people who don't stand strong against evil are like springs that have been polluted or pools that have turned dirty and muddy *(ERV 29:8)*. Hopes placed in mortals die with them; all the promise of their power comes to nothing *(NIV 11:7)*. A righteous person giving in to the wicked is like a contaminated spring or a polluted fountain *(CEB 25:26)*.

THE CHALLENGE

Highlight the key words or themes that stand out most to you in these scriptures.

_____
_____
_____
_____
_____
_____
_____
_____
_____
_____
_____

CHARACTER OF THE NATURAL/CARNAL

You're Wicked—I
What does the book of Proverbs say?

The Lord's views on being Wicked

There are six things the LORD hates, seven that are detestable to him: a heart that devises wicked schemes, feet that are quick to rush into evil *(NIV 6:16, 3:32)*, a mind devising wicked plans, feet that are quick to do wrong *(GW 6:18)*. False witness, breathing out untrue words, and one who lets loose violent acts among brothers *(BBE 6:19)*. He who justifies the wicked and he who condemns the righteous are both alike an abomination to the Lord *(ESV 17:15)*.

The Lord is far from the wicked *(ESV 15:29)* for He hates evil-minded people *(GNT 11:20)* and the way evil people live *(ERV 15:9)*. For evil designs are disgusting to the Lord *(BBE 15:26)*. God over throweth the wicked for their wickedness *(KJV 21:12)* and the Lord condemns those who plan evil *(GNT 12:2)*. The Lord will intentionally ignore the desires of a wicked person *(GW 10:3)* and he hates the offerings of the wicked *(ERV 15:8)*. The curse of the Lord is on the house of the evil-doer *(BBE 3:33)*. A person who is devious in his ways despises the Lord *(GW 14:2)*. If you say, "Look, we didn't know about it," the one who weighs hearts—doesn't he understand? The one who protects your life—he knows. He makes people pay for their actions *(CEB 24:12)*. The Lord has made everything for his purpose, even the sinner for the day of evil *(BBE 16:4)*.

THE CHALLENGE

Highlight the key words or themes that stand out most to you in these scriptures.

_____

_____

_____

_____

_____

CHARACTER OF THE NATURAL/CARNAL

You're Wicked—II
What does the book of Proverbs say?

Their Attitude

The wicked is those who find pleasure in doing wrong and who enjoy senseless evil *(GNT 2:14)*. They have abandoned a righteous life to live in the darkness of sin *(GNT 2:13)*. Their paths are crooked. Their ways are devious *(GNT 2:15)*.

The name of the wicked will rot *(CSB 10:7)* and he who pursues evil will die *(ESV 11:19)*. The wicked only want to deceive you *(GNT 12:5)* and to find evil things to do *(GNT 12:12)*. They desires evil; he has no consideration for his neighbor *(CSB 21:10)*. They look for ways to harm: others; even their words burn with evil *(GNT 16:27)*. They act disgustingly and disgracefully *(CSB 13:5)* because acting justly is dreaded by those who do evil *(CEB 21:15)*. Evil men have no knowledge of what is right *(BBE 28:5)* so they walk a crooked path *(GNT 21:8)* and have to pretend as best they can *(CSB 21:29)*. The wicked run away when no one is chasing them *(NLT 28:1)* and they squander their money on sin *(NLT 10:16)*. They accept secret bribes to pervert justice *(NLT 17:23)*. Sin disgraces a people *(CEB 14:34)*.

Do they not err that devise evil *(ASV 14:22)*? And foolish behaviour is round the head of the unwise *(BBE 14:24)*. The straight path is disgusting to the wicked *(CEB 29:27)* and they are trapped by evil desires *(NIV 11:6)* and the way of the wicked is like deep darkness; they do not know what makes them stumble *(NLT 4:19)*.

THE CHALLENGE

Highlight the key words or themes that stand out most to you in these scriptures.

_____

_____

_____

CHARACTER OF THE NATURAL/CARNAL

You're Wicked—III
What does the book of Proverbs say?

Their Tongue

The mouth of fools feedeth on folly *(ASV 15:14)* and the mouths of wicked people pour out a flood of evil things *(GW 15:28)*. A wicked man listens to evil lips; a liar pays attention to a malicious tongue *(NIV 17:4)*.
Evil is the person who speaks devious things *(GW 2:12)* and evil hides behind the words of the wicked *(CEB 10:11)*. For their words are a death trap *(CEB 12:6)*. The mouth of the wicked conceals violence *(ESV 10:6, 10:20)*. With their mouths the godless destroy their neighbors *(NIV 11:9)*. Worthless, wicked people go around telling lies *(GNT 6:12)* for the tongue that deceives will be cut off *(NLT 10:31)*. Gossip is spread by wicked people; they stir up trouble and break up friendships *(GNT 16:28)*. Those with crooked hearts won't prosper, and those with twisted tongues will fall into trouble *(GNT 17:20)*.

THE CHALLENGE

Highlight the key words or themes that stand out most to you in these scriptures.

_____

_____

_____

_____

_____

_____

_____

_____

CHARACTER OF THE NATURAL/CARNAL

You're Wicked—IV
What does the book of Proverbs say?

Actions upon others

The merciful acts of the wicked are cruel *(CSB 12:10)*. The upright man gives attention to the cause of the poor: the evil-doer gives no thought to it *(BBE 29:7)*. The bloodthirsty hate the upright *(KJV 29:10)*. A corrupt witness makes a mockery of justice; the mouth of the wicked gulps down evil *(NLT 19:28)*. To impose a fine on a righteous man is not good, nor to strike the noble for their uprightness *(ESV 17:26)*. Someone guilty of murder is digging his own grave as fast as he can. Don't try to stop him *(GNT 28:18)*. Evil people seek only rebellion; a cruel messenger will be sent against them *(CEB 17:11)* so if you've been foolish and arrogant, if you've been scheming, put your hand to your mouth *(CEB 30:32)*.

THE CHALLENGE

Highlight the key words or themes that stand out most to you in these scriptures.

_____
_____
_____
_____
_____
_____
_____
_____
_____

CHARACTER OF THE NATURAL/CARNAL

You're Wicked—V
What does the book of Proverbs say?

Consequences for being Wicked - A

[23] A fool finds pleasure in wicked schemes. [24] What the wicked dread will overtake them [25] When the storm has swept by, the wicked are gone [26] As vinegar to the teeth and smoke to the eyes, so are sluggards to those who send them. [27] but the years of the wicked are cut short. [28] but the hopes of the wicked come to nothing. [29] The way of the Lord is the ruin of those who do evil. [30] the wicked will not remain in the land. [31] but a perverse tongue will be silenced. [32] the mouth of the wicked only what is perverse *(NIV 10:23-32)*, but the wicked are brought down by their own wickedness, for they have nothing but trouble *(GNT 12:21)* and they can expect to be defeated by God's anger *(NCV 11:23)* for wickedness is the road to death *(GNT 12:28)* and the downfall of sinners *(GNT 13:6, 27:12)*.

The way of the faithless is their ruin *(CEB 13:15)* and they will be fully repaid for their ways *(NIV 14:14)* for they are brought down by their own wickedness *(NIV 11:5)*. Trouble follows sinners everywhere *(GNT 13:21, 11:8, 24:16)*. In the steps of an evil man there is a net for him *(BBE 29:6)*. There is much food in the ploughed land of the poor; but it is taken away by wrongdoing *(BBE 13:23)*. They have empty stomachs *(CEB 13:25)*. The wicked are thrown down by their own evil *(CEB 14:32)* and when they arrive, contempt, shame, and disgrace are sure to follow *(NLT 18:3)*. Those who have no respect for the law give praise to the evil-doer *(BBE 28:4)*.

THE CHALLENGE

Highlight the key words or themes that stand out most to you in these scriptures.

_____

_____

_____

_____

_____

CHARACTER OF THE NATURAL/CARNAL

You're Wicked—VI
What does the book of Proverbs say?

Consequences for being Wicked – B

Schemers are hated *(CEB 14:17)* and treacherous people are destroyed by their dishonesty *(NLT 11:3)* and the way of the wicked leads them astray *(NIV 12:26)*. The evil deeds of a wicked man ensnare him; the cords of his sin hold him fast *(NLT 5:22)*. They fall by their own wickedness *(GW 11:5)*. Deceit is in the heart of those whose designs are evil *(BBE 12:20)*. Whoever derides their neighbor has no sense *(NIV 11:12)*. Wicked people do not really gain anything *(GNT 11:18)*. Certainly, an evil person will not go unpunished *(GW 11:21)* how much more will the wicked person and the sinner receive their reward here on earth *(GW 11:31)*! Sudden disaster and destruction comes to the wicked *(ERV 3:25)* but men with warped minds are despised *(NIV 12:8)*. The lamp of wicked people will be snuffed out *(GNT 13:9)* they will be removed from the land, and the treacherous will be destroyed *(NLT 2:22)*. If you repay evil for good, evil will never leave your house *(NLT 17:13)* and the house of the wicked will be destroyed *(ESV 14:11)*. He will die for lack of discipline, led astray by his own great folly *(NLT 5:23)*. Whoso causeth the righteous to go astray in an evil way, he shall fall himself into his own pit *(KJV 28:10, CEB 26:27)* and those who roll a stone will have it turn back on them *(CEB 26:28)*. The violence of the wicked shall sweep them away, because they refuse to do justice *(ASV 21:7)*. Evil men will bow down in the presence of the good, and the wicked at the gates of the righteous *(NIV 14:19)*. The wicked are a ransom for the righteous; the treacherous will be punished in the place of the virtuous *(CEB 21:18)*. In the paths of the wicked lie thorns and snares *(NIV 22:5)*.

THE CHALLENGE

Highlight the key words or themes that stand out most to you in these scriptures.

_____

_____

CHARACTER OF THE NATURAL/CARNAL

You're Wicked—VII
What does the book of Proverbs say?

Effects on communities

People with no regard for others can throw whole cities into turmoil *(GNT 29:8)*. A city is brought to ruin by the words of the wicked *(GNT 11:11)* and when the wicked take charge, people go into hiding *(NLT 28:12)*. Overthrow wicked people, and they are no more *(GW 12:7,12:13)*. When the wicked dominate, the people moan *(CEB 29:1-2)*. When the wicked perish, there are shouts of joy *(CEB 11:10)* and when they rise and become numerous, so do crimes and men hide themselves *(ERV 28:28, CEB 29:16)*. But when the wicked perish, the righteous increase *(ERV 28:28)* and will see their downfall *(CEB 29:16)*.

Correcting Wicked People
Do not reprove a scoffer, or he will hate you *(ESV 9:8)*. Whoever instructs the cynic gets insulted; whoever corrects the wicked gets hurt *(CEB 9:7)*.

Financial Gain for the Wicked
Treasures of wickedness profit nothing *(ASV 10:2)* for in the profits of the sinner there is trouble *(BBE 15:6)*. The offering of evil-doers is disgusting: how much more when they give it with an evil purpose! *(BBE 21:27)*; so the wealth of sinners will go to the righteous *(GNT 13:22)*.

THE CHALLENGE

Highlight the key words or themes that stand out most to you in these scriptures.

_____

_____

_____

_____

_____

CHARACTER OF THE NATURAL/CARNAL

You're Wicked—VIII
What does the book of Proverbs say?

Don't be led by Wicked People

My son, if sinful men entice you, do not give in to them. *(NIV 1:10)*. If they say, "Come along with us; let's lie in wait for innocent blood, let's ambush some harmless soul; *(NIV 1:11)* let's swallow them alive, like the grave, and whole, like those who go down to the pit; *(NIV 1:12)* we will get all sorts of valuable things and fill our houses with plunder; *(NIV 1:13)* cast lots with us; we will all share the loot"— *(NIV 1:14)* my son, do not go along with them, do not set foot on their paths; *(NIV 1:15)* for their feet rush into evil, they are swift to shed blood *(NIV 1:16)*. How useless to spread a net where every bird can see it *(NIV 1:17)*! These men lie in wait for their own blood; they ambush only themselves! *(NIV 1:18)*. Such are the paths of all who go after ill-gotten gain; it takes away the life of those who get it. *(NIV 1:19)*. Do not plan to do something wrong to your neighbor while he is sitting there with you and suspecting nothing *(GW 3:29)*. When he winks with his eyes, he is planning to do wrong. When his lips are tightly closed, he is up to no good *(NIRV 16:30)*. You wicked one, do not lie in ambush at the home of a righteous person. Do not rob his house *(GW 24:15)*.

THE CHALLENGE

Highlight the key words or themes that stand out most to you in these scriptures.

_____

_____

_____

_____

_____

_____

CHARACTER OF THE NATURAL/CARNAL

Your Words have the power to Wound
What does the book of Proverbs say?

The tongue can kill life *(NLT 18:21)* and thoughtless words can wound as deeply as any sword *(GNT 12:18)*, an unkind answer will cause more anger and *(NCV 15:1)* cruel words crush your spirit *(GNT 15:4)*.

THE CHALLENGE

Highlight the key words or themes that stand out most to you in these scriptures.

_____

_____

_____

_____

_____

_____

_____

_____

_____

_____

_____

_____

_____

CHARACTER OF THE NATURAL/CARNAL

You Worry
What does the book of Proverbs say?

An anxious heart weighs a man down *(NIV 12:25)* and a troubled heart breaks the spirit *(CEB 15:13)*.

THE CHALLENGE

Highlight the key words or themes that stand out most to you in these scriptures.

_____

_____

_____

_____

_____

_____

_____

_____

_____

_____

_____

_____

_____

CHARACTER OF THE NATURAL/CARNAL

UNHEALTHY EMOTIONS OF THE CARNAL MAN

Abandoned, Abused, Accused, Adrift, Afraid, Aggravated, Aggressive
Animosity, Annoyed, Antagonistic, Anxious, Apathetic, Apprehensive, Argumentative
Baffled, Banished, Barren, Bashful, Beaten Down, Befuddled, Belittled
Blue, Boastful, Bored, Brokenhearted, Bugged, Burdened, Burned Up
Cheapened, Cheated, Childish, Clingy, Clumsy, Competitive, Compromised
Contentious, Contradictory, Contrary, Controlled, Covetous, Cowardly, Cranky
Cynical, Debased, Deceitful, Deceived, Defamed, Defeated, Defensive
Demeaned, Demoralized, Dependent, Depraved, Depreciated, Depressed, Deprived
Devalued, Devastated, Difficult, Disappointed, Discarded, Disconcerted, Discouraged
Distant, Distorted, Distressed, Distrustful, Disturbed, Dominated, Doomed
Empty, Enraged, Envious, Estranged, Exasperated, Excluded, Exhausted
Finished, Flighty, Flustered, Foggy, Forgetful, Forgotten, Forlorn
Fuming, Furious, Gloomy, Grieved, Grim, Grouchy, Guilty
Heartless, Helpless, Hesitant, Hindered, Hopeless, Horrible, Horrified
Immobilized, Impaired, Impatient, Impotent, Impoverished, Imprisoned, Impulsive
Indignant, Ineffective, Inefficient, Inept, Inferior, Inflexible, Infuriated
Isolated, Jealous, Jittery, Joyless, Judgmental, Jumpy, Lacking
Lost, Lousy, Low, Mad, Malicious, Maligned, Manipulated
Misunderstood, Misused, Mixed Up, Mocked, Moody, Mortified, Mournful
Obsessed, Obstinate, Obstructed, Offended, On Edge, Opiniated, Opposed
Panicky, Paralyzed, Paranoid, Peculiar, Perfectionistic, Perplexed, Persecuted
Punished, Puny, Pushed, Put Down, Puzzled, Rattled, Rebellious
Responsible, Restless, Restrained, Restricted, Ridiculed, Risky, Rotten
Scorned, Seething, Shaky, Shallow, Shameful, Shocked, Shot Down
Small, Smothered, Smug, Sorrowful, Spiteful, Stagnant, Stifled
Stumped, Stupid, Suffering, Suicidal, Superficial, Superior, Suspicious
Troubled, Turned Off, Unable, Unappreciated, Uncertain, Uncomfortable, Undecided
Unmindful, Unorganized, Unpleasant, Unprotected, Unreasonable, Unsettled, Unsure
Vengeful, Vexed, Vicious, Vindictive, Violated, Violent, Vulnerable
Wrong, Yearning

Agitated, Agony, Alarmed, Alienated, Alone, Aloof, Ambivalent, Anguished
Arrogant, Ashamed, At Fault, Attacked, Avoiding, Awful, Awkward, Bad
Belligerent, Bereft, Betrayed, Bewildered, Bitter, Blaming, Bleak, Blocked
Captive, Careless, Cast Off, Censured, Chagrined, Chaotic, Chastened, Cheap
Compulsive, Conceited, Condemned, Confined, Conflicted, Confounded, Confused, Contemptible
Crazy, Crippled, Critical, Criticized, Cruel, Crushed, Cursed, Cut Off
Defiant, Deficient, Defiled, Deflated, Degenerate, Degraded, Dejected, Demanding
Derided, Desecrated, Deserted, Desolate, Despair, Desperate, Destitute, Destroyed
Discredited, Disgraced, Disgusted, Dismal, Dismayed, Disorganized, Disparaged, Dissatisfied
Doubtful, Down, Downcast, Drained, Dread, Dreary, Embarrassed, Embroiled
Exploited, Exposed, Failure, Faithless, Fatigued, Fearful, Feeble, Filthy
Forsaken, Fragmented, Frantic, Fretful, Friendless, Frightened, Frigid, Frustrated
Gullible, Harassed, Hardened, Harsh, Hasty, Hatred, Haughty, Haunted
Hostile, Humiliated, Hurried, Hurt, Hypocritical, Hysterical, Ignorant, Immature
In a Bind, Inadequate, Incapable, Incensed, Incompetent, Inconsiderate, Inconsistent, Indecisive
Inhibited, Insecure, Insignificant, Insincere, Insulted, Intimidated, Irresponsible, Irritable
Left Out, Let Down, Limited, Listless, Livid, Lonely, Lonesome, Longing
Manipulative, Materialistic, Mean, Melancholy, Minimized, Miserable, Miserly, Mistreated
Muddled, Naive, Narrow, Nauseated, Negative, Neglected, Nervous, Obnoxious
Oppositional, Oppressed, Outcast, Outraged, Overlooked, Overwhelmed, Overworked, Pained
Perturbed, Pessimistic, Phobic, Phony, Pitiful, Powerless, Prejudiced, Pressured
Regretful, Rejected, Remorseful, Remote, Reproved, Repulsive, Resentful, Resistant
Ruined, Rushed, Ruthless, Sad, Sarcastic, Scared, Scattered, Scoffed At
Shunned, Shy, Sick, Sinful, Slammed, Slandered, Slighted, Slow
Stingy, Stressed, Stubborn, Tense, Terrible, Terrified, Thoughtless, Threatened
Tactless, Tearful, Temperamental, Thwarted, Timid, Tired, Tortured, Trapped
Undesirable, Undisciplined, Uneasy, Unforgivable, Unforgiving, Unfriendly, Unhappy, Unimportant
Unthankful, Unwanted, Unwise, Unworthy, Upset, Uptight, Used, Useless
Washed Up, Wasted, Weak, Weepy, Withdrawn, Worried, Worthless, Wounded

CHARACTER OF THE NATURAL/CARNAL

THINGS TO KEEP DOING

Character Transformation Reflection: What do you need to keep doing in order to prayerfully ask God to help you accept and adopt the scriptures outlined in this chapter as a measure of your faith, trust, belief and obedience to the Lord, for yourself, and to others?

_____

_____

_____

_____

_____

_____

_____

_____

_____

_____

_____

_____

_____

_____

_____

_____

_____

_____

_____

CHARACTER OF THE NATURAL/CARNAL

THINGS TO START DOING

Character Transformation Reflection: What do you need to start doing in order to prayerfully ask God to help you accept and adopt the scriptures outlined in this chapter as a measure of your faith, trust, belief and obedience to the Lord, for yourself, and to others?

_____
_____
_____
_____
_____
_____
_____
_____
_____
_____
_____
_____
_____
_____
_____
_____
_____
_____
_____
_____
_____
_____

CHARACTER OF THE NATURAL/CARNAL

THINGS TO STOP DOING

Character Transformation Reflection: What do you need to stop doing in order to prayerfully ask God to help you accept and adopt the scriptures outlined in this chapter as a measure of your faith, trust, belief and obedience to the Lord, for yourself, and to others?

_____
_____
_____
_____
_____
_____
_____
_____
_____
_____
_____
_____
_____
_____
_____
_____
_____
_____
_____
_____
_____
_____

Your Relationship With Your Wife

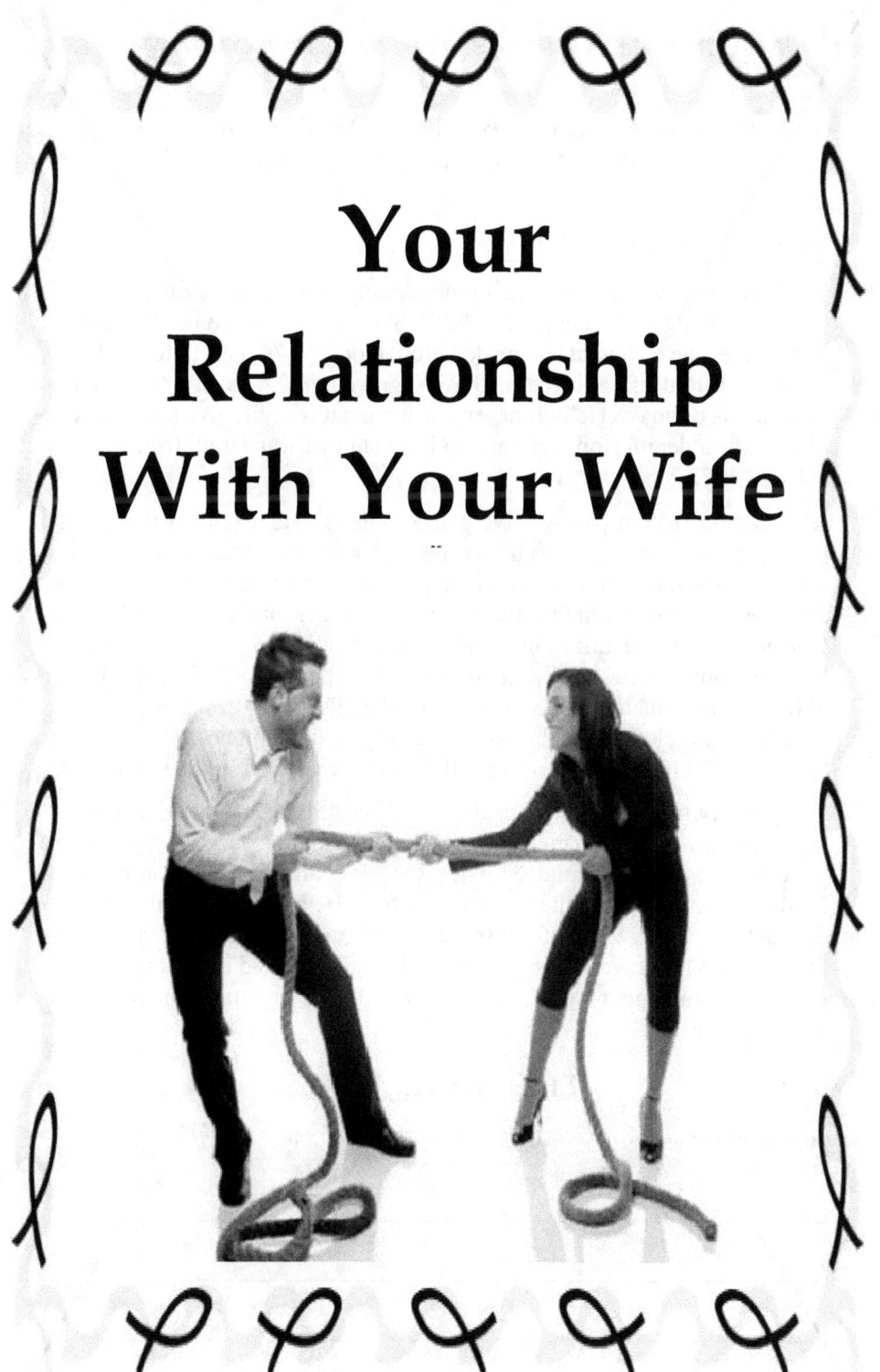

YOUR RELATIONSHIP WITH YOUR WIFE

You don't commit Adultery/You're Faithful—I
What does the book of Proverbs say?

Warning Against Adultery

Wisdom will save you from the immoral woman, from the seductive words of the promiscuous woman *(NLT 2:16)*. She has abandoned her husband and ignores the covenant she made before God *(NLT2:17)*. Entering her house leads to death; it is the road to the grave *(NLT 2:18)*. The man who visits her is doomed. He will never reach the paths of life *(NLT 2:19)*. As a bird that wandereth from her nest, so is a man that wandereth from his place *(KJV27:8)*.

(ERV 6:23-35) Your parents give you commands and teachings that are like lights to show you the right way. This teaching corrects you and trains you to follow the path to life. 24 It stops you from going to an evil woman, and it protects you from the smooth talk of another man's wife. 25 Such a woman might be beautiful, but don't let that beauty tempt you. Don't let her eyes capture you. 26 A prostitute might cost a loaf of bread, but the wife of another man could cost you your life. 27 If you drop a hot coal in your lap, your clothes will be burned. 28 If you step on one, your feet will be burned. 29 If you sleep with another man's wife, you will be punished.

30 A hungry man might steal to fill his stomach. If he is caught, he must pay seven times more than he stole. It might cost him everything he owns, but other people understand. 31 They don't lose all their respect for him. 32 But a man who commits adultery is a fool. He brings about his own destruction. 33 He will suffer disease and disgrace and never be free from the shame. 34 The woman's husband will be jealous and angry and do everything he can to get revenge. 35 No payment—no amount of money—will stop him.

THE CHALLENGE

Highlight the key words or themes that stand out most to you in these scriptures.

_____

_____

_____

_____

YOUR RELATIONSHIP WITH YOUR WIFE

You don't commit Adultery/You're Faithful—II
What does the book of Proverbs say?

The Wisdom of Avoiding Adultery

(ERV 5:1-20) Son, listen to this piece of wisdom from me. Pay attention to what I know to be true. ²Remember to live wisely, and what you learn will keep your lips from saying the wrong thing. ³Now, another man's wife might be very charming, and the words from her lips so sweet and inviting. ⁴But in the end, she will bring only bitterness and pain. It will be like bitter poison and a sharp sword. ⁵She is on a path leading to death, and she will lead you straight to the grave. ⁶Don't follow her. She has lost her way and does not even know it. Be careful. Stay on the road that leads to life. ⁷Now, my sons, listen to me. Don't forget the words I say. ⁸Stay away from the woman who commits adultery. Don't even go near her house. ⁹If you do, others will get the honor you should have had. Some stranger will get everything you worked years to get. ¹⁰People you don't know will take all your wealth. Others will get what you worked for. ¹¹At the end of your life, you will be sad that you ruined your health and lost everything you had. ¹²⁻¹³Then you will say, "Why didn't I listen to my parents? Why didn't I pay attention to my teachers? I didn't want to be disciplined. I refused to be corrected. ¹⁴So now I have suffered through just about every kind of trouble anyone can have, and everyone knows it." ¹⁵Now, about sex and marriage: Drink only the water that comes from your own well, ¹⁶and don't let your water flow out into the streets. ¹⁷Keep it for yourself, and don't share it with strangers. ¹⁸Be happy with your own wife. Enjoy the woman you married while you were young. ¹⁹She is like a beautiful deer, a lovely fawn. Let her love satisfy you completely. Stay drunk on her love, ²⁰and don't go stumbling into the arms of another woman.

THE CHALLENGE

Highlight the key words or themes that stand out most to you in these scriptures.

_____

_____

_____

_____

YOUR RELATIONSHIP WITH YOUR WIFE

You don't commit Adultery/You're Faithful—III
What does the book of Proverbs say?

Wisdom Will Keep You From Adultery

(ERV 7:1-27) My son, remember my words. Don't forget what I have told you. ² Consider my teaching as precious as your own eyes. Obey my commands, and you will have a good life. ³ Tie them around your finger. Write them on your heart. ⁴ Treat wisdom like the woman you love and knowledge like the one dearest to you.⁵ Wisdom will save you from that other woman, the other man's wife, who tempts you with such sweet words. ⁶ One day I was looking out my window ⁷ at some foolish teenagers and noticed one who had no sense at all. ⁸ He was walking through the marketplace and came to the corner where a certain woman lived. He then turned up the road that goes by her house. ⁹ The day was ending. The sun had set, and it was almost dark. ¹⁰ Suddenly, there she was in front of him, dressed like a prostitute. She had plans for him. ¹¹ She was a wild and rebellious woman who would not stay at home. ¹² She walked the streets, always looking for someone to trap. ¹³ She grabbed the young man and kissed him. Without shame, she looked him in the eye and said, ¹⁴ "I offered a fellowship offering today. I gave what I promised to give, ¹⁵ and I still have plenty of food left. So I came out to find you, and here you are! ¹⁶ I have clean sheets on my bed—special ones from Egypt. ¹⁷ My bed smells wonderful with myrrh, aloes, and cinnamon. ¹⁸ Come, let's enjoy ourselves all night. We can make love until dawn. ¹⁹ My husband has gone on a business trip. ²⁰ He took enough money for a long trip and won't be home for two weeks." ²¹ This is what the woman said to tempt the young man, and her smooth words tricked him. ²² He followed her, like a bull being led to the slaughter. He was like a deer walking into a trap, ²³ where a hunter waits to shoot an arrow through its heart. The boy was like a bird flying into a net, never seeing the danger he was in. ²⁴ Now, sons, listen to me. Pay attention to what I say. ²⁵ Don't let your heart lead you to an evil woman like that. Don't go where she wants to lead you. ²⁶ She has brought down some of the most powerful men; she has left many dead bodies in her path. ²⁷Her house is the place of death. The road to it leads straight to the grave.

THE CHALLENGE

Highlight the key words or themes that stand out most to you in these scriptures.

_____

_____

YOUR RELATIONSHIP WITH YOUR WIFE

You don't commit Adultery/You're Faithful - IV
What does the book of Proverbs say?

Everyone talks about how loyal and faithful he is, but just try to find someone who really is *(GNT 20:6)!* The mouth of an adulteress is a deep pit; he who is under the Lord's wrath will fall into it *(NIV 22:14)*. It is a danger to a man to say without thought, It is holy, and, after taking his oaths, to be questioning if it is necessary to keep them *(BBE 20:25)*. A faithful man shall abound with blessings *(KJV 28:20)*.

THE CHALLENGE

Highlight the key words or themes that stand out most to you in these scriptures.

_____

_____

_____

_____

_____

_____

_____

_____

_____

_____

_____

_____

YOUR RELATIONSHIP WITH YOUR WIFE

You Appreciate Her
What does the book of Proverbs say?

He who finds a wife finds what is good and receives favor from the Lord *(NIV 18:22)*. Fathers can give their sons an inheritance of houses and wealth, but only the Lord can give an understanding wife *(NLT 19:14)*.

THE CHALLENGE

Highlight the key words or themes that stand out most to you in these scriptures.

_____

_____

_____

_____

_____

_____

_____

_____

_____

_____

_____

_____

_____

Your Relationship with Your Wife

You see her as a crowning Glory
What does the book of Proverbs say?

He who finds a wife finds what is good and receives favor from the Lord *(NIV 18:22)* for a gracious woman is respected *(GNT 11:16)* and a wife of noble character is her husband's crown *(NIV 12:4)*.

THE CHALLENGE

Highlight the key words or themes that stand out most to you in these scriptures.

_____

_____

_____

_____

_____

_____

_____

_____

_____

_____

_____

_____

_____

YOUR RELATIONSHIP WITH YOUR WIFE

You're a Leader/Involved
What does the book of Proverbs say?

Her husband is well known, one of the leading citizens *(GNT31:23)*.

THE CHALLENGE

Highlight the key words or themes that stand out most to you in these scriptures.

_____
_____
_____
_____
_____
_____
_____
_____
_____
_____
_____
_____
_____
_____
_____
_____

YOUR RELATIONSHIP WITH YOUR WIFE

You Praise Her
What does the book of Proverbs say?

Her children stand and bless her. Her husband praises her *(NLT 31:28)* he says, "Many women are good wives, but you are the best of them all *(GNT 31:29)."*

THE CHALLENGE

Highlight the key words or themes that stand out most to you in these scriptures.

_____
_____
_____
_____
_____
_____
_____
_____
_____
_____
_____
_____
_____
_____
_____

YOUR RELATIONSHIP WITH YOUR WIFE

You Trust Her
What does the book of Proverbs say?

Her husband has full confidence in her and lacks nothing of value *(NIV 31:11)*.

THE CHALLENGE

Highlight the key words or themes that stand out most to you in this scripture.

_____

_____

_____

_____

_____

_____

_____

_____

_____

_____

_____

_____

_____

YOUR RELATIONSHIP WITH YOUR WIFE

You're Respected
What does the book of Proverbs say?

Her husband is respected at the city gate, where he takes his seat among the elders of the land *(GW 31: 23)*.

THE CHALLENGE

Highlight the key words or themes that stand out most to you in these scriptures.

_____
_____
_____
_____
_____
_____
_____
_____
_____
_____
_____
_____
_____
_____
_____
_____

YOUR RELATIONSHIP WITH YOUR WIFE

THINGS TO KEEP DOING

Character Transformation Reflection: What do you need to keep doing in order to prayerfully ask God to help you accept and adopt the scriptures outlined in this chapter as a measure of your faith, trust, belief and obedience to the Lord, for yourself, and to others?

_____

_____

_____

_____

_____

_____

_____

_____

_____

_____

_____

_____

_____

_____

_____

_____

_____

_____

_____

YOUR RELATIONSHIP WITH YOUR WIFE

THINGS TO START DOING

Character Transformation Reflection: What do you need to start doing in order to prayerfully ask God to help you accept and adopt the scriptures outlined in this chapter as a measure of your faith, trust, belief and obedience to the Lord, for yourself, and to others?

_____

_____

_____

_____

_____

_____

_____

_____

_____

_____

_____

_____

_____

_____

_____

_____

_____

_____

_____

YOUR RELATIONSHIP WITH YOUR WIFE

THINGS TO STOP DOING

Character Transformation Reflection: What do you need to stop doing in order to prayerfully ask God to help you accept and adopt the scriptures outlined in this chapter as a measure of your faith, trust, belief and obedience to the Lord, for yourself, and to others?

_____
_____
_____
_____
_____
_____
_____
_____
_____
_____
_____
_____
_____
_____
_____
_____
_____

Your Relationship With Your Husband

YOUR RELATIONSHIP WITH YOUR HUSBAND

You're a Blessing
What does the book of Proverbs say?

She brings him good, not harm, all the days of her life *(GW 31:12)*. Her children arise and call her blessed; her husband also, and he praises her *(NIV 31:28)* for it is better to live on the corner of a roof than to share a house with a nagging wife *(GNT 21:9)*.

THE CHALLENGE

Highlight the key words or themes that stand out most to you in these scriptures.

_____
_____
_____
_____
_____
_____
_____
_____
_____
_____
_____
_____
_____

YOUR RELATIONSHIP WITH YOUR HUSBAND

You're a Caretaker
What does the book of Proverbs say?

She watches over the affairs of her household *(NIV 31:27).*

THE CHALLENGE

Highlight the key words or themes that stand out most to you in this scripture.

_____
_____
_____
_____
_____
_____
_____
_____
_____
_____
_____
_____
_____

YOUR RELATIONSHIP WITH YOUR HUSBAND

You're Caring/Helpful
What does the book of Proverbs say?

Open thy mouth for the dumb in the cause of all such as are appointed to destruction *(GNT 31:8)*. Open thy mouth, judge righteously, and plead the cause of the poor and needy *(KJV 31:9)* so she opens her arms to the poor and extends her hands to the needy *(GW 31:20)*.

THE CHALLENGE

Highlight the key words or themes that stand out most to you in these scriptures.

_____
_____
_____
_____
_____
_____
_____
_____
_____
_____
_____
_____
_____
_____
_____

YOUR RELATIONSHIP WITH YOUR HUSBAND

You're Not a Nag
What does the book of Proverbs say?

A contentious wife is like constant dripping *(CSB 19:13);* it is better to live on the corner of a roofer in the wilderness than in a house with a contentious, angry or nagging woman *(CEB 21:9, 21:19).*

THE CHALLENGE

Highlight the key words or themes that stand out most to you in these scriptures.

_____

_____

_____

_____

_____

_____

_____

_____

_____

_____

_____

_____

_____

_____

YOUR RELATIONSHIP WITH YOUR HUSBAND

You're Discrete
What does the book of Proverbs say?

A woman who is beautiful but lacks discretion is like a gold ring in a pig's snout *(NLT 11:22)*.

THE CHALLENGE

Highlight the key words or themes that stand out most to you in these scriptures.

_____
_____
_____
_____
_____
_____
_____
_____
_____
_____
_____
_____
_____
_____
_____
_____
_____

YOUR RELATIONSHIP WITH YOUR HUSBAND

You Fear the Lord
What does the book of Proverbs say?

Charm is deceptive, and beauty is fleeting; but a woman who fears the Lord is to be praised *(NIV 31:30)*.

THE CHALLENGE

Highlight the key words or themes that stand out most to you in these scriptures.

YOUR RELATIONSHIP WITH YOUR HUSBAND

You're Gracious
What does the book of Proverbs say?

A gracious woman is respected *(GNT 11:16)*.

THE CHALLENGE

Highlight the key words or themes that stand out most to you in this scripture.

___

YOUR RELATIONSHIP WITH YOUR HUSBAND

You're Hard Working
What does the book of Proverbs say?

She considers a field and buys it; out of her earnings she plants a vineyard *(GW 31:16)*. She sets about her work vigorously; her arms are strong for her tasks *(GW 31:17)*. She sees that her trading is profitable, and her lamp does not go out at night *(GW 31:18)*. She makes linen garments and sells them, and supplies the merchants with sashes *(GW 31:24)*. She does not eat the bread of idleness *(GW 31:27)*.

THE CHALLENGE

Highlight the key words or themes that stand out most to you in these scriptures.

_____
_____
_____
_____
_____
_____
_____
_____
_____
_____
_____
_____

YOUR RELATIONSHIP WITH YOUR HUSBAND

You're Honorable
What does the book of Proverbs say?

Honor her for all that her hands have done, and let her works bring her praise at the city gate *(TNIV 31:31)*.

THE CHALLENGE

Highlight the key words or themes that stand out most to you in this scripture.

_____
_____
_____
_____
_____
_____
_____
_____
_____
_____
_____
_____
_____
_____
_____
_____

YOUR RELATIONSHIP WITH YOUR HUSBAND

You're Kind
What does the book of Proverbs say?

She openeth her mouth with wisdom; and in her tongue is the law of kindness *(KJV 31:26)*.

THE CHALLENGE

Highlight the key words or themes that stand out most to you in this scripture.

_____
_____
_____
_____
_____
_____
_____
_____
_____
_____
_____
_____
_____
_____
_____

YOUR RELATIONSHIP WITH YOUR HUSBAND

You're not Promiscuous—I
What does the book of Proverbs say?

Wisdom will save you from the immoral woman, from the seductive words of the promiscuous woman *(NLT 2:16)*. She has abandoned her husband and ignores the covenant she made before God *(NLT 2:17)*. Entering her house leads to death; it is the road to the grave *(NLT 2:18)*. The man who visits her is doomed. He will never reach the paths of life *(NLT 2:19)*. He who goes in the company of loose women is a waster of wealth *(BBE 29:3)*. For a loose woman is a deep hollow, and a strange woman is a narrow water-hole *(CEB 23:27)*. Yes, she is waiting secretly like a beast for its food, and deceit by her is increased among men *(CEB 23:28)*. A continual dropping in a very rainy day and a contentious woman are alike *(KJV 27:15)*, whosoever hideth her hideth the wind, and the ointment of his right hand, which bewrayeth itself *(KJV 27:16)*.

THE CHALLENGE

Highlight the key words or themes that stand out most to you in these scriptures.

_____

_____

_____

_____

_____

_____

_____

_____

_____

_____

YOUR RELATIONSHIP WITH YOUR HUSBAND

You're not Promiscuous—II
What does the book of Proverbs say?

(ERV 7:1-27) My son, remember my words. Don't forget what I have told you. ² Consider my teaching as precious as your own eyes. Obey my commands, and you will have a good life. ³ Tie them around your finger. Write them on your heart. ⁴ Treat wisdom like the woman you love and knowledge like the one dearest to you.⁵ Wisdom will save you from that other woman, the other man's wife, who tempts you with such sweet words. ⁶ One day I was looking out my window ⁷ at some foolish teenagers and noticed one who had no sense at all. ⁸ He was walking through the marketplace and came to the corner where a certain woman lived. He then turned up the road that goes by her house. ⁹ The day was ending. The sun had set, and it was almost dark. ¹⁰ Suddenly, there she was in front of him, dressed like a prostitute. She had plans for him. ¹¹ She was a wild and rebellious woman who would not stay at home. ¹² She walked the streets, always looking for someone to trap. ¹³ She grabbed the young man and kissed him. Without shame, she looked him in the eye and said, ¹⁴ "I offered a fellowship offering today. I gave what I promised to give, ¹⁵ and I still have plenty of food left. So I came out to find you, and here You're! ¹⁶ I have clean sheets on my bed—special ones from Egypt. ¹⁷ My bed smells wonderful with myrrh, aloes, and cinnamon. ¹⁸ Come, let's enjoy ourselves all night. We can make love until dawn. ¹⁹ My husband has gone on a business trip. ²⁰ He took enough money for a long trip and won't be home for two weeks.[a]"²¹ This is what the woman said to tempt the young man, and her smooth words tricked him. ²² He followed her, like a bull being led to the slaughter. He was like a deer walking into a trap, ²³ where a hunter waits to shoot an arrow through its heart. The boy was like a bird flying into a net, never seeing the danger he was in. ²⁴ Now, sons, listen to me. Pay attention to what I say. ²⁵ Don't let your heart lead you to an evil woman like that. Don't go where she wants to lead you. ²⁶ She has brought down some of the most powerful men; she has left many dead bodies in her path. ²⁷ Her house is the place of death. The road to it leads straight to the grave.

THE CHALLENGE

Highlight the key words or themes that stand out most to you in these scriptures.

YOUR RELATIONSHIP WITH YOUR HUSBAND

You're a Provider/Resourceful
What does the book of Proverbs say?

Every wise woman builds her house, but a foolish one tears it down with her own hands *(CSB 14:1)*. She selects wool and flax and works with eager hands *(GW 31:13)*. She is like the merchant ships, bringing her food from afar *(GW 31:14)*. She gets up while it is still night; she provides food for her family and portions for her female servants *(GW 31:15)*. In her hand she holds the distaff and grasps the spindle with her fingers *(GW 31:19)*. When it snows, she has no fear for her household; for all of them are clothed in scarlet *(GW 31:21)*. She makes coverings for her bed *(GW 31:22)*.

THE CHALLENGE

Highlight the key words or themes that stand out most to you in these scriptures.

_____
_____
_____
_____
_____
_____
_____
_____
_____
_____
_____

YOUR RELATIONSHIP WITH YOUR HUSBAND

You're Respected
What does the book of Proverbs say?

A gracious woman is respected *(GNT 11:16, 31:25)*, strong and not afraid of the future *(GNT 31:25)*.

THE CHALLENGE

Highlight the key words or themes that stand out most to you in these scriptures.

YOUR RELATIONSHIP WITH YOUR HUSBAND

You're Righteous
What does the book of Proverbs say?

She openeth her mouth with wisdom; and in her tongue is the law of kindness *(KJV 31:26)*.

THE CHALLENGE

Highlight the key words or themes that stand out most to you in this scripture.

YOUR RELATIONSHIP WITH YOUR HUSBAND

You're Strong
What does the book of Proverbs say?

She is strong and respected and not afraid of the future *(GNT 31:25)*.

THE CHALLENGE

Highlight the key words or themes that stand out most to you in this scripture.

_____

_____

_____

_____

_____

_____

_____

_____

_____

_____

_____

_____

_____

_____

_____

_____

YOUR RELATIONSHIP WITH YOUR HUSBAND

You're Trustworthy
What does the book of Proverbs say?

Her husband trusts her with all his heart, and he does not lack anything good *(GW 31:11).*

THE CHALLENGE

Highlight the key words or themes that stand out most to you in this scripture.

_____
_____
_____
_____
_____
_____
_____
_____
_____
_____
_____
_____
_____
_____
_____
_____

YOUR RELATIONSHIP WITH YOUR HUSBAND

You're Virtuous/Noble
What does the book of Proverbs say?

A prudent wife is from the Lord *(KJV 19:14)*. A wife of noble character who can find? She is worth far more than rubies *(GW 31:10)*, she is clothed in fine linen and purple *(GW 31:22)*, she is clothed with strength and dignity; she can laugh at the days to come *(GW 31: 25)*. "Many women do noble things, but you surpass them all" *(GW 31: 29)*. A gracious woman is respected, but a woman without virtue is a disgrace *(GNT 11:16)* and a virtuous woman is a crown to her husband: but she that maketh ashamed is as rottenness in his bones *(KJV 12:4)*.

THE CHALLENGE

Highlight the key words or themes that stand out most to you in these scriptures.

_____
_____
_____
_____
_____
_____
_____
_____
_____
_____
_____
_____

YOUR RELATIONSHIP WITH YOUR HUSBAND

THINGS TO KEEP DOING

Character Transformation Reflection: What do you need to keep doing in order to prayerfully ask God to help you accept and adopt the scriptures outlined in this chapter as a measure of your faith, trust, belief and obedience to the Lord, for yourself, and to others?

_____
_____
_____
_____
_____
_____
_____
_____
_____
_____
_____
_____
_____
_____
_____
_____
_____
_____
_____
_____

YOUR RELATIONSHIP WITH YOUR HUSBAND

THINGS TO START DOING

Character Transformation Reflection: What do you need to start doing in order to prayerfully ask God to help you accept and adopt the scriptures outlined in this chapter as a measure of your faith, trust, belief and obedience to the Lord, for yourself, and to others?

___

YOUR RELATIONSHIP WITH YOUR HUSBAND

THINGS TO STOP DOING

Character Transformation Reflection: What do you need to stop doing in order to prayerfully ask God to help you accept and adopt the scriptures outlined in this chapter as a measure of your faith, trust, belief and obedience to the Lord, for yourself, and to others?

_____
_____
_____
_____
_____
_____
_____
_____
_____
_____
_____
_____
_____
_____
_____
_____
_____
_____
_____
_____
_____

Your Relationship With Your Children

YOUR RELATIONSHIP WITH YOUR CHILDREN

You Discipline them with Physical/Verbal Correction
What does the book of Proverbs say?

If you love your children, you will correct them; if you don't love them, you won't correct them *(CEB 13:24)*. Spank him yourself, and you will save his soul from hell *(GW 23:14)*. Discipline your children and they will give you peace of mind and will make your heart glad *(NLT 29:17)*. Don't fail to correct your children. You won't kill them by being firm, and it may even save their lives *(CEB 23:13)*. Correction and discipline are good for children. If they have their own way, they will make their mothers ashamed of them *(GNT 29:15)* so correct your children before it's too late; if you don't punish them, you are destroying them *(CEB 19:18)*. Folly is bound up in the heart of a child, but the rod of discipline will drive it far away *(NIV 22:15)*.

THE CHALLENGE

Highlight the key words or themes that stand out most to you in these scriptures.

_____

_____

_____

_____

_____

_____

_____

_____

_____

_____

YOUR RELATIONSHIP WITH YOUR CHILDREN

You Leave an Inheritance
What does the book of Proverbs say?

The heritage of the good man is handed down to his children's children; and the wealth of the sinner is stored up for the upright man *(BBE 13:22)*.
House and riches are the inheritance of fathers *(KJV 19:14)*.
A wise servant shall have rule over a son that causeth shame, and shall have part of the inheritance among the brethren *(KJV 17:2)*.

THE CHALLENGE

Highlight the key words or themes that stand out most to you in these scriptures.

_____

_____

_____

_____

_____

_____

_____

_____

_____

_____

_____

_____

_____

YOUR RELATIONSHIP WITH YOUR CHILDREN

You Provide for their Physical Needs
What does the book of Proverbs say?

When it snows, she has no fear for her household; for all of them are clothed in scarlet *(GW 31: 21)*. She makes coverings for her bed *(GW 31: 22)*.

THE CHALLENGE

Highlight the key words or themes that stand out most to you in these scriptures.

_____
_____
_____
_____
_____
_____
_____
_____
_____
_____
_____
_____
_____
_____

YOUR RELATIONSHIP WITH YOUR CHILDREN

You Provide for their Spiritual Needs
What does the book of Proverbs say?

Those who fear the Lord are secure; he will be a place of refuge for their children *(NLT 14:26)*. The godly walk with integrity; blessed are their children who follow them *(NLT 20:7)*.

THE CHALLENGE

Highlight the key words or themes that stand out most to you in these scriptures.

YOUR RELATIONSHIP WITH YOUR CHILDREN

They Respect You
What does the book of Proverbs say?

Grandchildren are the crowning glory of the aged; parents are the pride of their children *(NLT 17:6)*.

THE CHALLENGE

Highlight the key words or themes that stand out most to you in this scripture.

_____
_____
_____
_____
_____
_____
_____
_____
_____
_____
_____
_____
_____
_____
_____

YOUR RELATIONSHIP WITH YOUR CHILDREN

You Teach/Train Them
What does the book of Proverbs say?

Train up a child in the way he should go: and when he is old, he will not depart from it *(KJV 22:6)*. Know your flock well; pay attention to your herds *(CEB 27:23)*, for no treasure lasts forever, nor a crown generation after generation *(CEB 27:24)*. When the grass goes away, new growth appears, and the plants of the hills are gathered *(CEB 27:25)*, then the lambs will provide your clothes, and the goats will be the price of your fields *(CEB 27:26)*. There will be enough goat's milk for your food, for the food of your house, and to nourish your young women *(CEB 27:27)*. Listen, my son, to your father's instruction and do not forsake your mother's teaching *(NIV 1:8, 4:1)*. They are a garland to grace your head and a chain to adorn your neck *(NIV 1:9)*. Listen, my son, and be wise, and keep your heart on the right path *(NIV 23:19)*. Young people who obey the law are wise; those with wild friends bring shame to their parents *(NLT 28:7)*. My son, if sinful men entice you, do not give in to them *(NIV 1:10)*. If they say, "Come along with us; let's lie in wait for innocent blood, let's ambush some harmless soul; *(NIV 1:11)* let's swallow them alive, like the grave, and whole, like those who go down to the pit; *(NIV 1:12)*. We will get all sorts of valuable things and fill our houses with plunder; *(NIV 1:13)* cast lots with us; we will all share the loot"— *(NIV 1:14)*. My son, do not go along with them, do not set foot on their paths; *(NIV 1:15)*. For their feet rush into evil, they are swift to shed blood *(NIV 1:16)*. How useless to spread a net where every bird can see it! *(NIV 1:17)*. These men lie in wait for their own blood; they ambush only themselves! *(NIV 1:18)*. Such are the paths of all who go after ill-gotten gain;   it takes away the life of those who get it. *(NIV 1:19)*.

THE CHALLENGE

Highlight the key words or themes that stand out most to you in these scriptures.

_____

_____

_____

_____

YOUR RELATIONSHIP WITH YOUR CHILDREN

THINGS TO KEEP DOING

Character Transformation Reflection: What do you need to keep doing in order to prayerfully ask God to help you accept and adopt the scriptures outlined in this chapter as a measure of your faith, trust, belief and obedience to the Lord, for yourself, and to others?

YOUR RELATIONSHIP WITH YOUR CHILDREN

THINGS TO START DOING

Character Transformation Reflection: What do you need to start doing in order to prayerfully ask God to help you accept and adopt the scriptures outlined in this chapter as a measure of your faith, trust, belief and obedience to the Lord, for yourself, and to others?

___
___
___
___
___
___
___
___
___
___
___
___
___
___
___
___
___
___
___
___
___
___
___
___
___
___

YOUR RELATIONSHIP WITH YOUR CHILDREN

THINGS TO STOP DOING

Character Transformation Reflection: What do you need to stop doing in order to prayerfully ask God to help you accept and adopt the scriptures outlined in this chapter as a measure of your faith, trust, belief and obedience to the Lord, for yourself, and to others?

_____
_____
_____
_____
_____
_____
_____
_____
_____
_____
_____
_____
_____
_____
_____
_____
_____
_____
_____
_____

Your Relationship With Your Parents

YOUR RELATIONSHIP WITH YOUR PARENTS

by being Diligent/Working Hard
What does the book of Proverbs say?

A wise youth harvests in the summer, but one who sleeps during harvest is a disgrace *(NLT 10:5).*

THE CHALLENGE

Highlight the key words or themes that stand out most to you in these scriptures.

_____
_____
_____
_____
_____
_____
_____
_____
_____
_____
_____
_____
_____
_____
_____

YOUR RELATIONSHIP WITH YOUR PARENTS

You Listen to Them
What does the book of Proverbs say?

Listen, my sons, to a father's instruction; pay attention and gain understanding *(NIV 4:1)*. Obey your father's commands, and don't neglect your mother's teaching *(NLT 6:20)*. Keep them ever folded in your heart, and have them hanging round your neck.*(BBE 6:21)*. *(ERV 6:23-35)*. Your parents give you commands and teachings that are like lights to show you the right way. This teaching corrects you and trains you to follow the path to life. In your walking, it will be your guide; when You're sleeping, it will keep watch over you; when You're awake, it will have talk with you *(BBE 6:22)*. For these commands are a lamp *(NLT 6:23)*.My son, if your heart becomes wise, I, even I, will be glad in heart *(CEB 23:15)*; and my thoughts in me will be full of joy when your lips say right things *(CEB 23:16)*.

THE CHALLENGE

Highlight the key words or themes that stand out most to you in these scriptures.

_____

_____

_____

_____

_____

_____

_____

_____

_____

_____

YOUR RELATIONSHIP WITH YOUR PARENTS

Being Righteous
What does the book of Proverbs say?

The proverbs of Solomon: A wise child brings joy to a father *(NLT 10:1, 17:25)*. The father of a righteous man has great joy; he who has a wise son delights in him *(NIV 23:24)*. Even children show what they are by what they do; you can tell if they are honest and good *(GNT 20:11)* because sensible children bring joy to their father *(NLT 15:20)*. If you love wisdom your parents will be glad *(CEB 29:3, 23:5)* and let her who gave you birth have joy *(CEB 23:5)*. My son, give me your heart, and let your eyes take delight in my ways *(CEB 23:26,* be wise, my child, and I will be happy; I will have an answer for anyone who criticizes me *(KJV 27:11)*.

However

It is foolish to ignore what your parents taught you *(GNT 15:5)*. The parent of a fool has grief, and the father of a godless fool has no joy *(GW 17:21, 19:13)*. There is nothing but sadness and sorrow for parents whose children do foolish things *(GNT 17:21)*. Foolish children despise their mother *(NLT 15:20)* and brings grief to her *(NLT 10:1, 17:25)*. He who is violent to his father, driving away his mother, is a son causing shame and a bad name *(BBE 19:26)* and if one curses his father or his mother, his lamp will be put out in utter darkness *(ESV 20:20)*

THE CHALLENGE

Highlight the key words or themes that stand out most to you in these scriptures.

_____

_____

_____

_____

_____

YOUR RELATIONSHIP WITH YOUR PARENTS

You Receive Their Correction/Discipline
What does the book of Proverbs say?

My child, listen when your father corrects you. Don't neglect your mother's instruction *(NLT 1:8)*. Don't make fun of your father or disobey your mother—crows will peck out your eyes, and buzzards will eat the rest of you *(CEB 30:17)* for what you learn from them will crown you with grace and be a chain of honor around your neck *(NLT 1:9)*. Wise children pay attention when their parents correct them, but arrogant people never admit they are wrong *(GNT 13:1, 15:5)* this teaching is a light, and the corrections of discipline are the way to life *(NLT 6:23)*.

THE CHALLENGE

Highlight the key words or themes that stand out most to you in these scriptures.

_____
_____
_____
_____
_____
_____
_____
_____
_____
_____
_____
_____

YOUR RELATIONSHIP WITH YOUR PARENTS

You Don't Steal From Them
What does the book of Proverbs say?

Whoso robbeth his father or his mother, and saith, It is no transgression; the same is the companion of a destroyer *(KJV 28:24)*.

THE CHALLENGE

Highlight the key words or themes that stand out most to you in this scripture.

_____
_____
_____
_____
_____
_____
_____
_____
_____
_____
_____
_____
_____
_____
_____
_____

YOUR RELATIONSHIP WITH YOUR PARENTS

You Take Care of Them
What does the book of Proverbs say?

Pay attention to your father, and don't neglect your mother when she grows old *(CEB 23:22)*.

THE CHALLENGE

Highlight the key words or themes that stand out most to you in this scripture.

_____
_____
_____
_____
_____
_____
_____
_____
_____
_____
_____
_____
_____
_____
_____
_____
_____

YOUR RELATIONSHIP WITH YOUR PARENTS

THINGS TO KEEP DOING

Character Transformation Reflection: What do you need to keep doing in order to prayerfully ask God to help you accept and adopt the scriptures outlined in this chapter as a measure of your faith, trust, belief and obedience to the Lord, for yourself, and to others?

YOUR RELATIONSHIP WITH YOUR PARENTS

THINGS TO START DOING

Character Transformation Reflection: What do you need to start doing in order to prayerfully ask God to help you accept and adopt the scriptures outlined in this chapter as a measure of your faith, trust, belief and obedience to the Lord, for yourself, and to others?

YOUR RELATIONSHIP WITH YOUR PARENTS

THINGS TO STOP DOING

Character Transformation Reflection: What do you need to stop doing in order to prayerfully ask God to help you accept and adopt the scriptures outlined in this chapter as a measure of your faith, trust, belief and obedience to the Lord, for yourself, and to others?

_____
_____
_____
_____
_____
_____
_____
_____
_____
_____
_____
_____
_____
_____
_____
_____
_____
_____
_____
_____

Your Relationship With Others

> Be courteous to all, but intimate with few, and let those few be well tried before you give them your confidence.
>
> George Washington

YOUR RELATIONSHIP WITH OTHERS

You Choose Them Wisely
What does the book of Proverbs say?

No one else can know your sadness, and strangers cannot share your joy *(NCV 14:10).* A righteous man is cautious in friendship, but the way of the wicked leads them astray *(NIV 12:26).* Walk with the wise and become wise; associate with fools and get in trouble *(NLT 13:20).* Follow the steps of good men instead *(NLT 2:20)* and don't associate with those who talk too much *(CEB 20:19, GW 11:13).* Don't befriend people controlled by anger; don't associate with hot-tempered people *(CEB 22:24)* and don't hang out with those who get drunk on wine or those who eat too much meat *(CEB 23:20).*

THE CHALLENGE

Highlight the key words or themes that stand out most to you in these scriptures.

_____
_____
_____
_____
_____
_____
_____
_____
_____
_____
_____

YOUR RELATIONSHIP WITH OTHERS

You're their Companion
What does the book of Proverbs say?

Walk with the wise and become wise; associate with fools and get in trouble *(NLT 13:20)*. As iron sharpens iron, so a friend sharpens a friend *(NLT 27:17)*. Don't desert your friend or a friend of your family; don't go to your relative's house when disaster strikes. Better a neighbor nearby than a relative far away *(CEB 27:10)*. There are "friends" who destroy each other, but a real friend sticks closer than a brother *(NLT 18:24)* because a friend is always loyal, and a brother is born to help in time of need *(NLT 17:17)*.

THE CHALLENGE

Highlight the key words or themes that stand out most to you in these scriptures.

YOUR RELATIONSHIP WITH OTHERS

You're Considerate
What does the book of Proverbs say?

A violent man enticeth his neighbour, and leadeth him into the way that is not good *(KJV 16:29)*. A wicked person desires evil; he has no consideration for his neighbor *(CSB 21:10)*. Do not plan to do something wrong to your neighbor while he is sitting there with you and suspecting nothing *(GW 3:29)*. Whoever derides their neighbor has no sense, but the one who has understanding holds their tongue *(NIV 11:12)*. Don't visit your neighbors too often, or you will wear out your welcome *(NLT 25:17)*.

THE CHALLENGE

Highlight the key words or themes that stand out most to you in these scriptures.

___

___

___

___

___

___

___

___

___

___

___

___

YOUR RELATIONSHIP WITH OTHERS

You Counsel Them
What does the book of Proverbs say?

The heartfelt counsel of a friend is as sweet as perfume and incense *(NLT 27:9)* as iron sharpens iron, so a friend sharpens a friend *(NLT 27:17)*.

THE CHALLENGE

Highlight the key words or themes that stand out most to you in these scriptures.

_____

_____

_____

_____

_____

_____

_____

_____

_____

_____

_____

_____

_____

_____

YOUR RELATIONSHIP WITH OTHERS

Your Helpful
What does the book of Proverbs say?

Do not withhold good from those who deserve it when it's in your power to help them *(NLT 3:27)*. If you can help your neighbor now, don't say, "Come back tomorrow, and then I'll help you." *(NLT 3:28)*.

__THE CHALLENGE__

Highlight the key words or themes that stand out most to you in these scriptures.

_____
_____
_____
_____
_____
_____
_____
_____
_____
_____
_____
_____
_____
_____
_____

YOUR RELATIONSHIP WITH OTHERS

You're Not Deceptive
What does the book of Proverbs say?

The kisses of an enemy are deceitful *(KJV 27:6)*. Like a crazy person shooting deadly flaming arrows *(CEB 26:18)* are those who deceive their neighbor and say, "Hey, I was only joking!" *(CEB 26:19)*. The wicked only want to deceive you *(GNT 12:5)*. People may cover their hatred with pleasant words, but they're deceiving you *(NLT 26:24)*. They pretend to be kind, but don't believe them. Their hearts are full of many evils *(NLT 26:25)* and a flattering mouth worketh ruin *(NLT 26:28)*. People who flatter their friends spread out a net for their feet *(CEB 29:5)*.

THE CHALLENGE

Highlight the key words or themes that stand out most to you in these scriptures.

_____

_____

_____

_____

_____

_____

_____

_____

_____

_____

_____

_____

YOUR RELATIONSHIP WITH OTHERS

You're Honest With Them
What does the book of Proverbs say?

Faithful are the wounds of a friend *(KJV 27:6)*.

THE CHALLENGE

Highlight the key words or themes that stand out most to you in this scripture.

_____

_____

_____

_____

_____

_____

_____

_____

_____

_____

_____

_____

_____

_____

YOUR RELATIONSHIP WITH OTHERS

You Don't Lie Against Them
What does the book of Proverbs say?

Do not testify spitefully against innocent neighbors; don't lie about them *(NLT 24:28).* [8] Don't be in a hurry to go to court. You might go down before your neighbors in shameful defeat. [9] So discuss the matter with them privately. Don't tell anyone else, [10] or others may accuse you of gossip. Then you will never regain your good reputation *(NLT 25:8-10).*

THE CHALLENGE

Highlight the key words or themes that stand out most to you in these scriptures.

_____

_____

_____

_____

_____

_____

_____

_____

_____

_____

_____

_____

_____

YOUR RELATIONSHIP WITH OTHERS

You Don't Lend or Borrow Money
What does the book of Proverbs say?

Securing Loans (Co-signing)

My child, have you promised to be responsible for someone else's debts *(GNT 6:1)*? Do not co-sign another person's note or put up a guarantee for someone else's loan *(NLT 22:26)*. If you can't repay, why should they be able to take your bed from you? *(CEB 22:27)*. If someone puts up security for a stranger, he will suffer for it, but the one who hates such agreements is protected *(CSB 11:15)*. Only someone with no sense would promise to be responsible for someone else's debts *(GNT 17:18)*. Take the garment of one who puts up security for a stranger; hold it in pledge if he does it for a wayward woman *(NIV 20:16)*.

Borrowing Money

Poor people are slaves of the rich. Borrow money and you are the lender's slave *(GNT 22:7)*. Have you been caught by your own words, trapped by your own promises? *(GNT 6:2)*. Well then, my child, you are in that person's power, but this is how to get out of it: hurry to him, and beg him to release you *(GNT 6:3)*. Don't let yourself go to sleep or even stop to rest *(GNT 6:4)*. Get out of the trap like a bird or a deer escaping from a hunter *(GNT 6:5)*.

THE CHALLENGE

Highlight the key words or themes that stand out most to you in these scriptures.

_____

_____

_____

_____

_____

YOUR RELATIONSHIP WITH OTHERS

You're Willing to Nurture Others
What does the book of Proverbs say?

A wise servant shall have rule over a son that causeth shame, and shall have part of the inheritance among the brethren *(KJV 17:2).*

THE CHALLENGE

Highlight the key words or themes that stand out most to you in this scripture.

_____
_____
_____
_____
_____
_____
_____
_____
_____
_____
_____
_____
_____
_____

YOUR RELATIONSHIP WITH OTHERS

You Value Them
What does the book of Proverbs say?

There are persons for companionship, but then there are friends who are more loyal than family *(CEB 18:24)* so don't desert an old friend of your family or visit your relatives when you are in trouble. A friend nearby is better than relatives far away *(CEB 27:10)*. Do not plan to do something wrong to your neighbor while he is sitting there with you and suspecting nothing *(GW 3:29)* and with their mouths the godless destroy their neighbors. Happy are those who are kind to the needy and their neighbors *(CEB 14:21)*.

THE CHALLENGE

Highlight the key words or themes that stand out most to you in these scriptures.

_____

_____

_____

_____

_____

_____

_____

_____

_____

_____

_____

_____

YOUR RELATIONSHIP WITH OTHERS

You're Not Violent
What does the book of Proverbs say?

A violent man enticeth his neighbour, and leadeth him into the way that is not good *(KJV 16:29)*.

THE CHALLENGE

Highlight the key words or themes that stand out most to you in thi scripture.

_____
_____
_____
_____
_____
_____
_____
_____
_____
_____
_____
_____
_____
_____
_____
_____

YOUR RELATIONSHIP WITH OTHERS

You're Words have the power to Wound
What does the book of Proverbs say?

With their words, the godless destroy their friends *(NLT 11:9)*.

THE CHALLENGE

Highlight the key words or themes that stand out most to you in this scripture.

_____
_____
_____
_____
_____
_____
_____
_____
_____
_____
_____
_____
_____
_____
_____
_____

YOUR RELATIONSHIP WITH OTHERS

THINGS TO KEEP DOING

Character Transformation Reflection: What do you need to keep doing in order to prayerfully ask God to help you accept and adopt the scriptures outlined in this chapter as a measure of your faith, trust, belief and obedience to the Lord, for yourself, and to others?

YOUR RELATIONSHIP WITH OTHERS

THINGS TO START DOING

Character Transformation Reflection: What do you need to start doing in order to prayerfully ask God to help you accept and adopt the scriptures outlined in this chapter as a measure of your faith, trust, belief and obedience to the Lord, for yourself, and to others?

YOUR RELATIONSHIP WITH OTHERS

THINGS TO STOP DOING

Character Transformation Reflection: What do you need to stop doing in order to prayerfully ask God to help you accept and adopt the scriptures outlined in this chapter as a measure of your faith, trust, belief and obedience to the Lord, for yourself, and to others?

_____
_____
_____
_____
_____
_____
_____
_____
_____
_____
_____
_____
_____
_____
_____
_____
_____
_____
_____
_____
_____
_____
_____
_____

A AGUIDE TO BO BY

FOLLOW JESUS

One day while her pastor Rev. Smith, her son Algie and I was sitting with her at the nursing home, she told us the story of how she asked God to give her a guide to go by. This is her story:

Jesus was walking as a nobody. Raggedy, nasty, and all these people sitting alongside the road was sad. They wasn't saying a word. They was just sitting there and so when He got along there, something said tell them a story something to make em laugh, and when he got through telling stories, they all followed him to Galilee and all of em joined the church. That's how the stories got started!

Rev. Smith asked her, "Sister, tell me again, you asked God to give you a guide to go by, and what he told yah?" She says "God told me

Follow Jesus every day
You follow him in the words you say
You follow him in the gifts you bring
Just follow him in everything
You follow Jesus in your prayers
Let him lead you everywhere
and he will choose a better way
If you will follow him each day
~ Momma VanHooose

MY GRANDMA'S ADVICE

You ask God, if there's something you want to know, He'll tell yah!

If someone don't believe you, tell them to ask God. He'll reveal it to them.

REFERENCES

Border: http://transasia.me/border-coloring-pages/border-coloring-pages-christian-border-horizontal-christian-fish-religious-borders-print-coloring-pages-free-border-coloring-pages/

George Washington Quote Retrieved (2014) VeryBestQuotes.com

Prayer image: Retrieved (2018) from:
https://www.pinterest.co.uk/jfayenichols22/clip-art/?lp=true

www.ingramcontent.com/pod-product-compliance
Lightning Source LLC
LaVergne TN
LVHW051548070426
835507LV00021B/2470